You spin me round

ALSO IN THE SERIES

Running feet, sharp noses: Essays on the animal world

In the good seats: Essays on film

You spin me round

Essays on music

PVA Books

First published in 2024 by PVA Books.

Edited by Adrian Duncan, Niamh Dunphy, Nathan O'Donnell

Editorial assistance by Jack Delaney, Sadbh O'Brien

Designed by Daly & Lyon, London

Printed in Germany by GGP Media GmbH, Pößneck

Copyright © 2024 individual contributors, Paper Visual Art Journal

Second printing, 2025; third printing, 2026

All rights reserved. No part of this publication may be reproduced in whole or in part in any form without prior written permission from the publisher.

Ciaran Carson's 'Marking Time' was originally published in *Last Night's Fun: A Book about Music, Food, and Time* (Jonathan Cape, 1996). Reproduced with permission of the Ciaran Carson Estate.

Wendy Erskine's 'Hot Legs' was originally published in *The Quietus*, February 2023. Reproduced with permission.

'Visions of Johanna', M J Harrison © 2023

ISBN 978-1-9161509-5-9

PVA greatly acknowledges the support of the Arts Council/An Chomhairle Ealaíon.

pva-books.com

CONTENTS

7 *Some Girls Are Bigger than Others*
Aingeala Flannery

17 *'O Superman' Laurie Anderson, 1981*
Declan Long

25 *Second Movement*
Colin Graham

39 *Adagio*
Jayne A. Quan

49 *'Pity the Meat': Notes on Iggy Pop*
Brian Dillon

61 *Marking Time*
Ciaran Carson

77 *Alien Lanes*
Peter Geoghegan

89 *Visions of Johanna*
M. John Harrison

97 *The Last Place that Felt like Home*
Sydney Weinberg

107 *Good Life*
McKenzie Wark

119 *Nostalgia, Ultra: Ennui and Excess in Late Nineties Suburbia*
Tabitha Lasley

129 *Hot Legs*
Wendy Erskine

141 Notes on Contributors

143 Image List

Some Girls Are Bigger than Others

Aingeala Flannery

I

Kenny Rogers is the best singer in the world. Better than Kris Kristofferson and Glen Campbell put together. There's a cassette player in our Ford Cortina and this is the stuff we listen to on our summer holiday, driving up the west coast from Kerry to Donegal. My mother chain-smokes Carroll's and threatens to kill us if we don't stop tormenting each other in the back seat. My little sister can't sit in the middle in case she gets sick, and my big brother can't sit there either because Daddy won't be able to see over his head. The road is a patchwork of potholes, tractors hide behind hairpin bends, and every time we go over a humpback bridge an acidic swell of chips and ice cream rises in my throat. 'Stop!' my sister screams. We pull in and my mother reefs her out the back of the car to vomit into a ditch of blazing orange montbretia. We take off again and my tailbone hurts from bouncing up and down on the middle hump – an injustice I'll endure so long as I'm in charge of the music. 'Put on Charley Pride,' my mother says to my father. She can't drive and won't touch anything on the dashboard for fear the car will swerve off the road. 'He's a beautiful singer,' she says. I slip the tape out of its case and hide it under her seat. Daddy catches my eye in the rear-view mirror, and says nothing. We both know Charley Pride is cat.

II

We've moved to Dublin and Daddy is after buying a 'music centre'. It has a twin tape deck, a radio, and a turntable. Down the road from our house, there's a newsagents called Tuthill's that sells records, comics, and the music magazine *Smash Hits*. I own two 7-inch singles: 'Heart of Glass' by Blondie and 'Kids in America' by Kim Wilde. On Sunday afternoons, I take the kitchen radio upstairs to listen and sing along to Jimmy Greeley's Top 30 show. My mother, sick of the racket, tells me she's heard farts that are better at holding a tune. I record myself singing 'Wonderful Tonight' and realise that she's right. I'm brutal. No one can ever know how brutal. I rewind the cassette and tape over the evidence. How ordinary my life is going to be. I will never represent Ireland in the Eurovision Song Contest. Or travel the world with a suitcase of spangly jumpsuits and stilettos. As the counter on the cassette recorder ticks over, I remember how two years earlier, I won a talent show in the town we used to live in. I stood on the community centre stage and sang an Elvis song, and a man, possibly a priest, presented me with a box of Black Magic chocolates. I thought I'd hit the big time. Now I know they just took pity on me, and I feel ashamed.

III

I join a disco dancing troupe that makes it into the finals of the Poparama National Disco Dancing Competition. Our leotards are blue. Our leg warmers are pink. Around our necks and waists we wear streamers that our mothers made from spools of ribbon and sequins they bought at Joan's fabric shop in Clondalkin village. To the synthesised drum beat of Anita Ward's disco anthem, 'Ring My Bell', we perform a routine that's a cross between 'The Siege of Ennis' and a military two-step, hopping in and out of formation like demented marionettes. We come second and there is no prize, but we get to meet Radio 2 DJs Ruth Buchanan and Barry Lang. At the end of the year, we're asked to perform our routine in a concert that'll also feature boys from St Joseph's National School. I've already outgrown my leotard. I have breasts and a camel-toe. I turn the wrong way during the routine and when I realise my mistake I run into the wings and hide behind a curtain, where I encounter a curly headed boy with a million freckles. He's holding a tin whistle. 'I can't do it,' he says, crying. I tell him I've made an absolute show of myself. For a few minutes, we stand in silence, staring uselessly at the audience of teachers and parents. The boy's name is Michael Christopher. A few years later, we're in the same gang that traipses up the Monastery Road to a field on the Naas dual carriageway, where we lie in the long grass, roll cigarettes, and talk about music. Later again, when he's a famous singer, he falls and suffers a fatal brain injury. They bury him in Newlands Cross Cemetery, in a grave opposite the one where we bury my father in the same year. Dad is dead at fifty-four. Mic Christopher at thirty-two.

IV

Echo and the Bunnymen are playing at the SFX. I'm a fourteen-year-old goth with a hairdressing regime that involves whipped egg white, constant back-combing, and an industrial haze of cheap hairspray. I wear Dr. Marten boots and an old man's Crombie. My mother has knitted me a massive black jumper that I never take off. If you really want to know, she hates me and I'm only allowed go to the concert if my brother goes too. Technically, the Bunnymen's new album belongs to him – he's out plumbing with my father and earns enough to buy records. He goes around in baggy jeans and a grey checked shirt that's too Big Country for my liking. Tonight, he's agreed to wear eyeliner and a crucifix in his ear. The only problem is I'll have to pierce his ear first. So here he is, sitting on a kitchen chair with a rolled-up tea towel between his teeth. After a couple of failed attempts to get the darning needle through his ear, the ice cube he's pressing against it has melted away to nothing. His flesh is meaty, much thicker than I expected, and there's a watery pink stream of blood running down his neck. It won't hurt as much if I do it fast. I wipe the lobe, find the puncture hole, and force the needle through. He grunts and bucks up off the chair. 'Fuck! Fuck! Fuck!' he slams his fist down on the kitchen table. His ear is still pumping when I put the crucifix in. I soak balls of cotton wool in Dettol and dab the wound, but the blood keeps coming, on the bus into town, on the walk to Sherrard Street, and at the concert as we sway and wave our arms, and shout and cheer to the Bunnymen – my brother bleeds like he's channelling Padre Pio. Tomorrow morning, the eyeliner will come off and the crucifix will come out. He's helping my father install a central heating system at a boarding school in Castleknock and the nuns wouldn't like it.

V

At the junction of Dame Street and South Great George's Street, beside the twenty-four-hour Centra, there's a strip club called Lapello. It is, by its own account, Dublin's longest established gentlemen's club. In my time-warped head, this place is still the Underground – a subterranean dive bar where new bands build up a following and the cost of entry is in or around a pound. On Monday nights, Teds from around the city converge here for a rock 'n' roll hop where Jumpin' George and Boppin' Billy play Gene Vincent, Eddie Cochran, and Buddy Holly records. At sixteen, or thereabouts, I start to frequent the Underground with a few of the Clondalkin Teds: one is a taxidermist and self-taught equestrian artist, another (my boyfriend) an apprentice carpenter with a pompadour quiff, brothel-creeper shoes, and a wardrobe of two-tone drape suits. I like their style. My father, however, does not approve of hops and he detests Teddy Boys. Where he grew up in Lancashire, they were switchblade-carrying layabouts who were after one thing only. So, he calls in a favour and gets me an occupation: making chips in Kentucky Fried Chicken on O'Connell Street. It means I'm in town every day and I'm earning enough money to go out. The Leaving Cert looms in the middle distance, but I'm much more interested in what's happening down in the Underground. With my Crombie buttoned up to cover my school jumper and camouflaged by a nimbus of cigarette smoke, I take sips from a glass of lager and lime. My favourite act is A House. Too clever to care about image, their songs 'Kick Me Again Jesus' and 'What a Nice Evening to Take the Girls up the Mountains' are loud and catchy. I go see them with my friend Colm, who warns me to hide my uniform as I cross the stage to get to the toilets because 'yer man, the guitarist, is in the guards'. Before the year is out, Colm gets a Green Card and emigrates to Wisconsin, and I get a third-round offer of arts in Maynooth. A House signs a record deal with Warner. The next time I see the singer, Dave Couse, we're working in the same radio station. He's presenting a music show and I'm reading the news. We chat in the staff kitchen. Me, waiting for the microwave to ping on a carton of soup. Him, making tea. 'Y'know,' I say. 'I went to your gigs in the Underground in my school uniform.' 'That's gas,' Dave says. He takes his mug of tea down to the studio. I eat the soup and go back to my desk to write the news. Whenever we meet, we stop to talk, and I always forget to ask him if the guitarist was really in the guards.

VI

I am in love with K. He has long black hair and his make-up is always perfect. I'm bunking off a lecture by a playwright whose fiery beard and temperament intimidate me. Instead, I lie in bed listening to *Secrets of the Beehive*, the new David Sylvian album with K. He calls me 'Ange' and talks to me about books and films and music. Prince is a genius. Gram Parsons is his favourite country singer. I think it's 'tragic' the Smiths have broken up. He says Morrissey needs Johnny Marr more than Johnny Marr needs Morrissey. K writes me letters and sends mixtapes in the post; he does his own cover art and writes the track lists in a spidery hand. Someday, he'd like to have his own record shop, but right now, he's on the dole. He'll probably pawn his bass guitar and move to London. On Saturdays, he sells bootleg tapes on O'Connell Bridge. The stock doesn't even belong to him. He's fucked if the guards catch him because they'll confiscate the tapes and he'll owe The Guy. 'Can't you make your own tapes?' I ask. And K explains how expensive it would be to buy a recorder, plus the cost of the concert tickets and the cassettes. Besides, The Guy would murder him. The thought of K's pale thin body washing up in Ringsend horrifies me. I wrap my arms and legs around him like a shield. But before long, he's recording gigs for The Guy. Sometimes I go along with K. It's easier for girls, the bouncers don't frisk you on the door. I put the recorder down the front of my tights. At a 10,000 Maniacs gig in the National Stadium, we forget to gaffer tape the 'on' light, and I've to keep my hands in my lap all night to cover the red beam shooting out of my gusset. K eventually grows tired of bootlegging and I grow tired of his existential despair. He takes the boat to London, where he gets a job with a record company and signs some of the biggest indie acts of the early nineties. Our paths cross briefly when I'm in a good place and K is not. Then, the century turns and for many years I don't hear any news of him. Eventually, technology enables us to find people, whether they want to be found or not, and I track K down to a quaint English town, where he's running his own record shop. He looks happy now, and I decide to leave him alone.

IN CONCERT

ECHO and the Bunnymen

S.F.X. CONCERT HALL
FRIDAY, 14th SEPTEMBER, 1984

Doors open 8.00 p.m.

ADMISSION — — — **£6.50**

Nº 309

To be retained
No refunds
No re-admission
Right of admission reserved

No Cameras, No Recorders, No Alcohol

'O Superman'
Laurie Anderson, 1981

Declan Long

Our way home was always the long way. Mum and Dad preferred the indirect route; the best bet, they thought, for dodging checkpoints, tailbacks, routine interrogations. Sunday evening, saying goodbye at the end of a day that always dragged – every few months, the same family visit to our two Derry aunts, the same welcome, the same warmth, the same afternoon of doing nothing, of staying inside whatever the weather, of seeing only what could be seen through the half-closed blinds – then taking off, waving through the rear window as we disappeared into the dark. First, the car would crawl across the top deck of the Craigavon Bridge ('Go slow! Go slow!' we chanted, my brother and sister and I), then pick up speed on the ascent out of town, veering north-east in line with the nearby river and the mostly invisible lough, tiny lights from the far side coming and going in the distance. For a while, somewhere beyond the suburbs, the three of us fell silent in the back, drifting into our own worlds as we gazed out on all the familiar, passing in-betweenness, too tired to talk, too tired to amuse or annoy each other. We were taking the long way, but taking nothing in, thinking only of our own movement, cruising through the pale glow and empty space of small, stern towns – Eglinton, Greysteel, Ballykelly – on and on towards larger places to be negotiated or bypassed – Ballymoney, Coleraine, Ballymena – keeping going, no pit stops at roadside shops, petrol stations, takeaways.

When we travelled, we prayed. Our parents insisted. As children, we found it entirely normal to mumble the hypnotic repetitions of the rosary, muttering our way through these mantras, these meditations on spiritual mysteries – joyful, sorrowful, and glorious – while bored in the backseat of our Mazda 323. For Mum and Dad, saying the rosary within the closed world of the moving car was a moment to proclaim our family's faith. (How many times did we hear the phrase 'the family that prays together stays together'?) But it was also, for the rest of us, a way of marking time. When we prayed, we counted. While our Mum's hands travelled from one small milestone to the next on the loop of her rosary beads, we counted in our heads. 'Hail Mary' *one*. 'Hail Mary' *two*. 'Hail Mary' *three*. 'Hail Marys' all the way to ten. Then one to ten again. And again.

∗

Well into the journey, Dad would turn on the radio. 'Let's just hear the headlines,' he'd say. Now and then, if a story stood out, he'd raise the volume. At other times, he'd lower the sound or switch it off – protecting us, perhaps, or protecting himself. We'd pester him to shift the dial from evening bulletins on Radio Ulster over to the chart show on Radio One. This was an essential Sunday ritual, at home or on the road: hearing the new Top 10, the ups and downs, the new entries, the new number 1. Listening wasn't easy in the car: poor-quality speakers, inconsistent signal. And on the last leg of our drive home – pressing on past one blacked-out field after another, skirting the edge of thick forests, climbing over higher ground – each of the week's hits would come and go through the hiss and haze of medium-wave. In the gaps between tracks, we waited for the breaking news of what would come next: the three of us hunched forwards, leaning into the waves of unstable sound, tilting towards the impassable gap between our parents in the front.

'O SUPERMAN'

＊

On 18 October 1981:

10. The novelty nostalgia of 'It's Raining' by Shakin' Stevens; in the back, we mimicked and mocked the pastiche '50s style, crooning into invisible microphones; in the front, Mum and Dad seemed pleased to hear 'a proper song'.

9. Elvis Costello's boring country ballad 'Good Year for the Roses'; what had happened, we wondered, to the geeky upstart who warned that Oliver's Army was 'on its way'?

8. An odd electronic ghost story, a song that largely passed us by: Godley & Creme's 'Under Your Thumb', something that surely felt eerie and cheerless in ways we couldn't connect with.

From 7 to 3: a spectrum of connection and disconnection, highs and lows.

7. The Jam's 'Absolute Beginners', a raucously melodic new entry, bolshy horn blasts and clanging Rickenbacker riffs pushing the car's speakers, and our parent's patience, to the limit; I was alone in falling for, and fighting for, this stroppy outburst about losing – 'like I do' – an era to daydreaming.

6. 'Open Your Heart' by the Human League; music that sounded expansive, propulsive, aerodynamic. To hear this inside the family car – looking through the windscreen at the dark road ahead – felt like being lifted off the ground; the soaring, precision-engineered sound taking us into the air, flying us home.

5. 'Happy Birthday' by Altered Images: giddy, delirious, and in our small world, instantly divisive.

4. 'Thunder in the Mountains' by Toyah. Back then, for a while, what a peculiar superstar she was: glamorous and preposterous. The song itself – in all its dopey New Romantic drama – was amiably rousing and ridiculous, tuneful enough to be liked, or at least tolerated, by everyone.

3. A different story, or a different version of the same story: 'The Birdie Song' by the Tweets, tuneful enough to be hated, really hated, by everyone. And yet, as we shrieked in mock-suffering – 'No! No! No!' – we laughed, really laughed, all of us, together.

∗

At number 2: something else, a new type of sound, as if the channel had been changed. It started – had it started? – as a single, repeating note, a lone voice. It was a type of breathing – quick, short, gasps, metronomically regular – and something other than breathing, something synthesised. We'd have guessed a broadcasting glitch, a stuck needle, except that, moments after, a second voice – singing, speaking, somewhere in between – uttered two words, intoning a name we knew:

O Superman ...

A plea across the airwaves, vocoder-fuzzy, at once heartfelt and robotic. If this was music, it was music from far away, an alien singer calling to an alien we knew. We weren't so much hearing a song – these mysterious breaths, this sorrowful voice – as overhearing a distant, intimate entreaty. We were listening in to something beyond us, something out there. Another word or another name, one we couldn't catch, was sing-song spoken (it was, I would later learn, 'O judge') before we were brought back to earth, back inside the car, back to ourselves. Tenderly, in descending notes, the voice sang to us, or to some of us, through the darkness:

Oh Mom and Dad ...

'Mom', with its American 'o'.

They looked at each other, our Mum and Dad, and we looked at them.

Again, the beats of the 'ah, ah, ah'. Seconds later, the lead voice synchronised with the panting rhythm – adding a layer, thickening the timbre, and changing the tone from prayerful concern to sarcastic laughter:

Ha Ha Ha Ha, Ha Ha Ha Ha, Ha Ha ...

We laughed in return: uncertain, unnerved. All of us, listening and laughing. For Mum and Dad, this was not music. For the rest of us, it was not *our* music, not the music of the Sunday evening countdown. For me, beginning to find my own way, it was not *my* music, there was nothing here – nothing yet – I could fall for or fight for. This song about Superman, or 'Mom and Dad', or something else: it seemed like a joke we didn't get. Unlike most of the chart hits we were drawn to at that time, these unearthly, half-human voices were not guiding us along familiar emotional paths. This hardly there music was not expressing sentiments we could name. We had an awareness of *feelings* – but feelings that clashed, overlapped, blurred. If the song's opening was a 'verse', it was also the opening of a multiverse, spinning us into an unstable version of reality.

O Superman ... Oh Mom and Dad ...

Quiet now, we listened as each line led somewhere new. An answering-machine message: the owner of this voice *is not home right now*. Then a call from a concerned mother, a chorus of birdsong rising as she asks *but are you coming home?* Then the same voice, but in a different guise, a new character, issuing a stark warning about *the incoming planes*.

✳

In the distance, glimpsed through trees and hedgerows: lights from the town, lights from the harbour, lights around the lough. We were close to home – coming down from higher ground.

That night, there were no delays. On the last stretch of the drive, Dad turned down the volume; he was tired – and tired of a song that made no sense. He would raise the level again when the number 1 came on – 'It's My Party' by Dave Stewart and Barbara Gaskin. We'd managed a clear run home – no doubt our prayers had worked. Out there on our part of planet Earth, others were praying too. It had been the hardest of years. At ten years old, I understood very little. Local news came to us in fragments. News from beyond came barely at all. I was learning to listen closely, to live quietly. In the background, for a long time, the volume low: the sound of breathing, breathing, breathing.

Second Movement

Colin Graham

It begins with two hard, definite notes on the violins, played *fortissimo* (very loud), *senza sordino* (unmuted), and *allegro* (fast). The First Movement has just finished – more than twenty novelistic minutes contemplating something dark, anxious, maybe hopeful, but certainly a bit fearful. It has ended with a faltering solo piccolo, the frailest sound in the orchestra. Now the remnants of that tiny sound and its single voice – standing, diminished, alone – are swept away by the force and terror of a music that will not be stopped.

Melodies are passed around the orchestra at frantic speed. The strings play at a sickening off-beat. The snare drum enters with military force. Now it's like a march – but as if a march were a mood or an insistent pattern of thought – and bass notes are added that come up through your feet. There's a pause, a gathering and then an explosion of crashes, a series of crescendos, the snare drum is back, the timpani, the brass like an army going into battle, and then another pause and then a brutal conclusive flourish. The whole thing takes about four minutes. It's terrifying and sickening. It's buttonholing. You're trapped in a corner, with no escape. It's the monologue of a massive ego, with no room for anything but its own echoing mania. It's on the verge of violence. And yet, it's thrilling because it's loud, fast, almost comic, and it sounds a bit, somehow, folkish. It is driven by the knowledge of something dark and irresistible that it cannot look in the eye.

I was a teenager in a house that was not musical. Neither of my parents had been to secondary school beyond the age of fourteen. I was the first on either side of the family to go to university. At grammar school in the first year, we were told to rest our heads on the desks, close our eyes, listen to Grieg's 'Morning Mood' from the Peer Gynt Suite and imagine a Norwegian sunrise over the fjords. It was kind of nice music but it sounded worlds away – not just in a different country but from a different class. It was alien to me as a sound and I had no idea what Norway was supposed to look like (years later I'd realise the piece is actually set in the Moroccan Sahara). I did have an inkling that there was something transcendent in the music and that I was being tested on my ability to hear it. I couldn't hear it.

That felt like a failing in me. But I could hear plenty in the Jam, the Who, Small Faces, Two Tone, and Bob Marley. Mod music made me a dandy of sorts and reading poetry at school, and then out of school, exaggerated the variety of styles I tried out. As my intellectual life falteringly developed, I was reading Keats in search of a profundity that his words wouldn't reveal, and dressing like I was in a Merchant Ivory film (not entirely without jeopardy in 1980s Belfast). And I was listening over and over to the one classical music cassette I'd bought – Beethoven's Symphony No. 6, 'Pastoral'. I kind of got this. The storm, the cuckoo, the shepherds. The housing estate I lived in ended at our back garden and beyond that there were fields and cows. The smell of slurry and tattered Union Flags was probably not what Beethoven had in mind, but I could begin to layer the 'Pastoral' over the green fields and I could hear the tunes and feel that it was all very powerful. It still felt like it belonged to the world of the posh kids at school and it couldn't shake me away from the Kinks. On and off through my adult years, I'd listen to classical music. I went to the Proms several times with a cultured girlfriend when I worked for a summer in London. Berg's Violin Concerto was a highlight – those awful, lonely first notes on open strings – but each time I heard classical music, I left it behind.

SECOND MOVEMENT

Elgar's Cello Concerto became another passing favourite. And one year, for no particular reason, I decided to go to hear it live at the National Concert Hall. It was played before the interval and it was fine, but nothing like the famous Jacqueline Du Pré recording. Dmitri Shostakovich's Symphony No. 10 was after the interval. All I knew about him were the Jazz Suites. Slight and silly pieces, it seemed, but pleasant enough. And then everything changed when I entered the sound world of Shostakovich's intense, jokey, unreadable music, full of the quotation and allusion of someone who can't or isn't able to say things directly. That's when I first experienced the power of the Second Movemer of Symphony No. 10 in E Minor, op. 93. The programme notes said the movement was 'a musical portrait of Stalin', who had died the year in which Symphony was composed. I became obsessed with this man, his music, and his life.

Shostakovich died in 1975. It is amazing to think that my life can have overlapped with someone who, as a child, as he sometimes told people, had seen Lenin arrive by train in St Petersburg in 1917. In the first part of his creative life, Shostakovich was a product of that period, the revolutions of 1905 and 1917. His early revolutionary fervour took him towards experimentation with form and sound. He earned a living for a time as a cinema pianist and, the rumour goes, lost his job because he was laughing too much to play the music to accompany Charlie Chaplin movies. His early symphonies are playful and joyous, always ready to try new things.

Shostakovich's tendency to push boundaries eventually meant that (along with other Russian composers and artists) his version of revolutionary art would run counter to the cultural orthodoxies that were put in place under the Stalin regime. Shostakovich's early opera *The Nose* (based on Gogol's story) was denounced as elitist and anti-proletarian. His 1934 opera, *Lady Macbeth of Mtsensk*, was seen by Stalin; subsequently, an article entitled 'Muddle Instead of Music' appeared in *Pravda* in response to the opera, supposedly written by Stalin himself, again accusing him of 'formalism' – that is, not writing music in the Soviet style, to the glory of the revolution and the proletariat, but being bourgeois and under foreign influence. The article said that things might 'end very badly' for such a composer. Shostakovich was in trouble. Julian Barnes's novel about the composer, *The Noise of Time* (2016), dramatises the idea that during this period he kept a suitcase of clothes by his front door so that, if called on by the KGB during the night, he would not disturb his family as he was taken away.

Shostakovich rehabilitated himself explicitly with his Symphony No. 5, first performed in 1937 and subtitled 'A Soviet Artist's Response to Just Criticism'. His recantation is hard to hear in the music because he has learned to write in a way that allows the state to hear what it expects (triumphalism and hopefulness) while, at the same time, the individual in that state can, perhaps, hear something more dissonant, melancholy, and sardonic. Shostakovich's rehabilitation means making an ambiguous music; this characterises the remainder of his public work, with two sides always evident – the stalwart of the state/the secret 'formalist' and individualist – in varying equations and balances, with no critic ever quite able to pin him down.

During the Siege of Leningrad, he composed the extraordinary Symphony No. 7. It was premiered in 1942 in Leningrad by an orchestra who were incapable of playing it, partly because many of the best musicians in the city had died and partly because those who were left in Leningrad were starving. (The one time I saw it performed, a trumpet player collapsed on stage because of the effort involved in playing it.) It begins with a long First Movement, buoyant and gentle at the beginning and then eddying into something a little more assertive. This builds to what's known as the 'invasion theme' – a theme that starts out on strings, gathers force around the orchestra, and ends up as a scarifying depiction of an army on the march, both physically and ideologically. For its first listeners, it was obvious that the relentless and 'total' sound of the end of the first movement of Symphony No. 7 was a musical account of the ideas and the hardware of Nazi totalitarianism, which, at the time of its premiere, was still laying siege to Leningrad. But it is music, after all, and a depiction of a naïve tune that morphs into an unremitting militarism as a definitive ideology, is not necessarily fixed in place. To Shostakovich's embarrassment, the Symphony made him world famous. He appeared on the cover of *Time* wearing a Leningrad fireman's helmet. He was sent, reluctantly, after the war, to the US as a cultural ambassador of the USSR, on the strength of the popularity of Symphony No. 7. There are accounts of his fear as Western journalists press him on the ideological restrictiveness of the Stalinist state, and I often think this anxiety is caused by his knowledge that his musical critique of totalitarianism can work (and was meant to work) both ways.

It's raining in West Cork. The holiday home smells damp and uncared for. We've been coming to the same place for years and each year it declines a little more. The montbretia are hanging low in the wind and the fuschias are dripping and miserable. Shostakovich's music is in my head constantly now, as a mystery to be solved. I've found, to the increasing dismay of my children, that if I press play on the Second Movement of the Symphony No. 10 in the car as we leave the house for the drive to their school in the morning, it will finish its adrenalin-inducing gallop just as we arrive at the school gates. The boys quickly grow weary of this start to the day.

There's something in Shostakovich's music that has caught me, but I can't pin it down. Maybe it's the same reason why, at the age of twenty, I wanted to study communist writing in Britain between the wars – that attempt to turn the materials of the lived world and of socialism as an idea into an effective aesthetic experience. Though is that what Shostakovich is doing? He seems both less earnest and more serious than Orwell or Auden. There's a photograph of him laughing hysterically in the crowd at a football match. It's the only happy photo of him I can find. MacNeice was more a rugby man and it's hard to imagine Auden at a spectator sport less highbrow than opera. I still don't understand Shostakovich's music or his politics.

As the summer rain falls in West Cork, we're high enough up a hill to be enveloped by the clouds and taken further away from the quotidian world. Our annual holiday here has become a time when I know I can read something for its own sake – not work, not 'research', not preparing for the year ahead. In this unreal, detached, and temporary place of retreat I find myself marking passage after passage in Solomon Volkov's *Testimony: The Memoirs of Dmitri Shostakovich*. Actually, this book is not quite 'by' Solomon Volkov, it's 'as related to and edited by Solomon Volkov'. Published in 1979, *Testimony* is one of my favourite books. It may be a true account of Shostakovich's life, told to Volkov in private. Or it may be one of the greatest scams in biographical writing, the work of a fantasist. Scholars disagree. I read it for its energy, which derives from its absolute conviction that Shostakovich was an anti-Stalinist who only just got away with it. He was, according to Volkov, a *yurodivy*, a long-standing figure in Russian culture who begins as a kind of holy fool and then becomes something like a joker, a truth-sayer to kings, a jester whose words and meanings are enveloped in such layers of irony that they can no longer be fully understood. The role is intended to unsettle.

For Volkov, Shostakovich's music, especially when Stalin was alive, is anti-Stalinist and anti-totalitarian, but never explicitly so. Shostakovich, the man who laughed at Chaplin, is laughing, darkly, at Stalin, and at the Stalinist state. According to Volkov, it is only in *Testimony* that this truth can be revealed. The key moment in Volkov's book is when Stalin dies in 1953. The pressure is suddenly released. Shostakovich is writing his Symphony No. 10 – the symphony is premiered at the end of that year. Of the Second Movement, Volkov 'quotes' this from Shostakovich:

> I couldn't write an apotheosis to Stalin, I simply couldn't. I knew what I was in for when I wrote the Ninth. But I did depict Stalin in music in my next symphony, the Tenth. I wrote it right after Stalin's death, and no one has yet guessed what the symphony is about. It's about Stalin and the Stalin years. The second part, the scherzo, is a musical portrait of Stalin, roughly speaking.

So there it is. That intense and fervid Second Movement, which I'd heard in the concert hall when I'd gone to hear Elgar's World War I melancholic cello, turned out, according to Volkov, to be Shostakovich dancing on Stalin's grave, using the orchestra to replicate the pathologies of Stalin's personality. (The Second Movement is in 2/4 time, so it zips along, but that's also the time signature of Georgian dance music, including the sabre dance, which the movement replicates in its increasing tempo – Stalin was, of course, from Georgia.) The Second Movement is so horrifying because it is the outpouring of years of fear about the personality of Stalin, under whom Shostakovich had suffered and to whom he'd often been called close.

Volkov's Shostakovich is a man released at the end of his life (when most of the conversations that make up the book are supposed to have taken place) from the bonds of fealty he knew he had to pay to the Party. Volkov's Shostakovich is witty, sharp, and oppressed, and finds his creativity redirected from modernist experimentation to complex and restrained irony in music, always on the edge of giving himself away and daring his listeners to say it. There's certainly evidence for this – for instance, years after his death, Shostakovich's work *Learner's Manual* (also known as *Antiformalist Rayok*) was first performed. It set the speeches denouncing him and other composers at the post-Zhdanov conferences in 1948 to parodic party and folk tunes.

And yet ... Volkov's book set Shostakovich definitively over and against the Soviet state. It's more complicated. Shostakovich's next symphony, No. 11 (1957), is known as 'The Year 1905'. It looks back with unmitigated pride on the revolution of that year, and includes another sickening piece of music that represents the Tsar's forces attacking the revolutionaries. (Shostakovich's family were more 1905 than 1917 people.) Even here, though, there's the potential for the attack on the revolutionaries of 1905 to be heard as a critique of the Russian invasion of Hungary in 1956. It's always complicated.

*

After the summer holiday, my obsession takes a new turn. I learn that Shostakovich was awarded an honorary degree by Trinity College Dublin (TCD) in 1972, and so I make an appointment with the Manuscripts and Archives Department of the Library to visit their reading space, through and beyond the Long Room, to sift through the scant documents about the visit. I'm embarrassingly nervous about seeing this material. It feels like it's bringing me closer to Shostakovich himself. If I meet anyone I know in the Manuscript Room, I'm not sure that I'll be able to explain why I'm here.

The archive boxes are delivered to my desk. They include a very smart summary of Shostakovich's career, for the attention of the Provost, written by composer Brian Boydell. There's a photo of

Shostakovich in his TCD gown at the ceremony, and there's a photo of Shostakovich at the Boydells' house, with various people, including – I can't quite believe this – Professor Jacqueline Hill from the History Department in my university. Her husband was Professor of Russian in TCD in the 1970s and acted as interpreter. She later gives me a copy of the photo and points to a man in a leather jacket. 'KGB, of course.' She tells me that, in person, Shostakovich was nervous and polite. I've read that he deliberately took the longest and slowest boat journey he could find to get to Dublin (via London) because he knew the KGB would put him on and meet him off the boat on either end, but, for the journey itself, he'd be briefly free of their surveillance.

As I sit in the Manuscript Room reading the accounts of the visit (Shostakovich later sent £100 to TCD: 'May this money be my modest participation in the expenses of building the student hostel'), music strikes up outside. Tomorrow Boston College is due to play against Georgia Tech in an American football game at the Aviva. The Boston College marching band is in the quad at Trinity, in full regalia and at full volume playing marching tunes, tunes to bond over, music to set you, without wavering, on one side of a battle with absolute conviction. Music of the Party, music in a cause.

I study Shostakovich's face in the photograph, which was taken just outside the room I'm sitting in, in the Trinity quad in 1972. His look is anxious, quizzical, wary, and wise. I imagine him transposed to the present moment, observing the Boston College band and hearing their relentlessly upbeat partisanship. In doing so, something about his music clarifies for me. Volkov sees Shostakovich as an individual pitted against the state, someone who has to hide his individuality to survive and can only confess this to Volkov, as it were, posthumously. But listening to the Boston College band and inhabiting that look of Shostakovich's, I see something else, something that helps me make sense of his paradoxes as well as my own over-interest in him.

I remember with vividness, as I sit in the Manuscript Room, the sound of flutes and drunken voices singing from forty years before. By the time I was a teenager, the Eleventh Night bonfire had moved to the field behind our house. It was a wild, raucous, bacchanalian evening and night of loyalist bonding, which I'd gone to with fear, trembling, and excitement, having helped build the bonfire for years. But as a teenager it began to appal me. The songs, the flute music, the hatred that is soaked into the music and the people who participate became, at that moment, unbearable. So as I sat in my bedroom as a fifteen-year-old on the evening of the eleventh of July, the posters on my bedroom walls (The Specials, The Who, postcards of Pre-Raphaelite paintings, Shakespeare's portrait, pictures of heavily adorned Vespas) were flickering and aglow with the flames of the bonfire and the room was filled with the beating, insistent music of sectarian history – drums hit with fury, like an explosion; the sound of the flute, not as a pastoral pastime but as a military call to march – the very kind of music the Second Movement of Symphony No. 10 parodies; the music that represents both who Shostakovich was, as a child of the revolution, and what oppressed him. That look on his face in the photograph reminds me that he was never a Party man and never not a Party man, that his music emerges from both the fear and the pleasure that ideological conviction can bring to human life and from which we cannot, as individuals, disentangle ourselves. I sat on my bed as a fifteen-year-old, revolted by the sounds outside, fully convinced that I could never believe in or participate in what I heard. But I was part of it, and part of me was still thrilled by it, just as Shostakovich knew he was part, not just of Russia, but of its revolution, even the elements of it that wanted to annihilate him. It's why his 'portrait of Stalin' is so powerful – because in his hatred of Stalin there is intimate understanding; there is terror; there is no escape; there is heart-racing anxiety and wild, compromised pleasure.

Adagio

Jayne A. Quan

Our spare closet is a space where I hide discarded hobbies and past failures. It's a graveyard of parts and old tech for tinkering, pristine product boxes I think will serve a new purpose, heaps of fabric I've yet to find a use for. It's stuffed with charging cables and wires, a surplus of books we can't get rid of, and boxes of things we've never unpacked.

I recently dug through photo equipment and poster rolls to produce a slim black box, tucked behind unworn formal attire and sitting on top of a badly sunken box of college textbooks. It was my old flute.

The flute was not my forte. At this point in my life, no instrument really is. I've happily played in community symphonies in San Francisco and New York;

however, if you asked me if I played well, I would say that I knew when strategically *not* to play so as not to interfere with the sound of my more talented companions. I emphasise *community* symphonies because they required no audition, just a joy for playing. In any case, I started my musical journey playing the flute. And I continued my musical journey playing the trumpet. One of many transitions in my life.

The slim black box no longer had a handle – it had fallen off years ago and was replaced with a clever shoulder strap. A piece of orange electrical tape was still stuck to the outside, declaring my name in a style of handwriting I hadn't used since I was a pre-teen. The flute itself was tarnished, in need of a thorough polish, but it still played, if I could play it.

I didn't really want to play it.

I wanted to look at it. I wanted to align my fingers against the keys, feel the shape and weight of the cool metal. I didn't really want to play it, but I pursed my lips and produced a note anyway. And even though it had been many years since I had last pressed this instrument to my mouth, my brain and my fingers produced a memory I didn't know I could still access.

While attending UCD, I had a room that overlooked the Elm Park Golf & Sports Club. I'd positioned my desk to always face the green. I would play Max Richter's 'On the Nature of Daylight' on repeat while trying to etch out words for poems and writing about my brother and about my transition. I'd occasionally try my hand at short stories, but mostly, I returned to writing about my brother. Now, when the song comes on, I see the golf course, the wet sidewalk, the gate that separated the club from the residential street that I lived on. I see my brother, the ghost of him and his smile. I am riding through the cycle of time, between the strings of instruments, in between one note and the next.

Sometimes I hear something and it feels so familiar. I know I should be able to place it, but it never comes. Not everything is a perfect recall – sometimes things sit at the precipice of knowing and I am haunted for days by the particular twang of a single chord or remnants of a harmony. If I could just fill in more texture, more nuance, more sound stage or instrumentation or even the next note, perhaps I could unlock the rest of the melody.

But sometimes it simply does not come, and I have to wait for the shadow to pass on its own.

I ran through scales on the flute, up and down: first chromatic, then major, and then minor. I tried to circle through fifths, but both my fingers and my memory stalled after just three scales. I wasn't surprised I could still play. That sounds like bragging, but if you can blow a note out of the neck of a beer bottle, you can technically play the flute.

ADAGIO

Though I *have* played in ensembles as an adult, I haven't done so in years. I haven't touched any of my instruments, really. The reason why they end up in the closet of neglected hobbies: I don't have enough time. If it was important to me, I could make the time – couldn't I? Not enough hours in the day, except that there are for the things one *wants* to do. It's why the neglected hobbies become revisited hobbies, why the closet is a state of reorganisation, why things in there rotate, shuffle from the back to the front and back again.

I like to do things I call 'hands busy, head empty' tasks. They're a way to unwind without much mental calculation. Playing an instrument doesn't count. It requires my hands to be busy and my head to be very full. Reading and playing music is an exercise in translation, taking lines and dots and turning them into another language.

I was tired. My head was already very full, and I had no texts to translate into melodies. My busy hands could only take me so far in this excavation. My pursed lips and lungs could only interpret so much. I remembered some of the songs I used to play on this instrument, could hum my parts, but there was too much distance between my present and my past.

Where did all that time go?

How could I try to remember?

*

I received a message on Instagram telling me that he had died. Just an innocuous social-media notification, like anything else. A ping and he's gone.

I instantly (morbidly) imagined his coffin. My high-school music teacher was so tall that he would duck his head when walking through doorways. He was hard to miss – over 190 cm with brilliant orange hair and a big goofy smile. He had the proportions of one of those inflatable dancing balloons in front of car dealerships. Did they make special coffins for extremely tall, lanky folks who were more noodle-shaped than human-shaped?

He was the kind of teacher people formed lasting memories of, like how he would get so tired of us looking at the clock just above his head that he eventually covered the whole thing with tape. Or when he wore a giant sun hat that made him look even bigger and goofier during summer band practices outside, otherwise he would turn as red as a lobster after just one morning. I think band teachers know that they teach social outcasts, weirdos who turn to band for comradery and shelter from the more popular kids. He made being weird feel very normal, like we were the ones our peers had to catch up to. For him, being goofy and being kind were synonymous with one another – he didn't care what we did in our personal lives, around campus or after school, as long as what we did made us happy, better people.

When I left high school, we kept in touch. He played on a soccer team in the evenings with his wife, and I would watch their games and get to know her, and she would ask me how college was going. He would invite me to come back to campus to run sectionals for the trumpets during summer practices. He gave me cash afterwards, and even though he was apologetic that it wasn't much, he was still trying to be my teacher. Don't do something you're good at for free.

But, slowly, my visits became less frequent.

I hadn't seen him since before the pandemic. He still taught at the same high school I tried my best to avoid. He loved seeing alumni and was very happy for a visit, often snapping a photo and posting it to his Facebook timeline after a meet-up. We did not snap a photo when I saw him last.

I had just come back from Ireland. He was always surprised to see me, but he was always surprised to see any alumni. I told him how I'd been. I said that I was dating a teacher and I would love for him to meet her someday.

Between one visit and my last, I had transitioned. Was that the surprise on his face? Should I have brought it up? I didn't know how to. I don't think he cared, really. After all, I was a happy, better person.

Even though time expanded between my visits, he was a very important person in my life at a very peculiar time. He was a beacon for the social outcasts in my high school. When I say he was my band teacher, I don't just mean that I took one band class. My schedule sometimes had two or three band classes during a single semester. I was involved in after-school music productions, marching-band practices, and before-school extracurricular ensembles that he supervised. Like other band geeks, I stayed on campus long after the final bell rang, either for practice or in the time leading up to events (if you're early, you're on time; if you're on time, you're late; and if you're late, it's unacceptable).

Though I retained very little of the formal music theory I learned, the life lessons this man taught me continue to help me – I don't have to do it, I get to do it; non-verbal communication can be just as valuable as something spoken; move with a purpose, et cetera. The last one followed me off the football field and crept into other aspects of my life as I got older. He used to say it to us when our steps looked lazy, when we didn't quite hit our mark in time, or when we didn't snap into a stationary hold. But then I started using it to navigate busy city sidewalks, purposefully sidestepping slower walkers and cutting a line through herds of tourists with ease in Manhattan. Eventually, it made itself into broader, grander aspects of my life. I thought of it when planning my career, when I made the decision to go forward with a medically assisted transition, when I planned to pursue a writing degree in Dublin. Whatever I do, however I move, I move with a purpose.

Anybody *could* have given me these lessons. But he taught them alongside the music.

There was a part of me that was so scared of rejection by bringing up my transition that the only coping mechanism I could logically pursue was to create distance. And distance was easy when all one had to do was stop visiting their high-school music teacher.

Truthfully, I thought he'd be there forever.

I thought I could keep putting off that conversation for another year, continuously reshuffling him in my life, so that I could revisit my high school's campus when I no longer felt so much shame.

∗

I sat on the floor, slim black box cracked open, silver tarnished flute pieced together. Arvo Pärt's 'Spiegel im Spiegel' played loudly from my speakers. I had recently rediscovered the song and it had crawled into my ear and burrowed into my brain and now I was playing it, trying to connect me and the man who had just died through time, through the space between one note and the next.

The British composer Alex Heffes put 'Spiegel im Spiegel' on the *Dear Frankie* soundtrack in 2004 – one of my favourite films at the time. He would go on to compose the soundtrack to *11.22.63* in 2016, a TV mini-series about the assassination of John F. Kennedy on that very date. Part of the same subject for the *New York Times*' 2011 short Op-Doc *The Umbrella Man*, which opens with the first notes to 'Spiegel im Spiegel' and which I would see for the first time in 2023: the year my favourite teacher died.

Time is a flat circle. The nature of daylight is that it continuously gives way to but also breaks darkness. The golf course and my brother's ghost. The band room and my music teacher's smile.

I sat on the ground playing simple scales from a flute I hadn't touched in years because I was trying to intertwine my life like a Möbius strip, trying to make two parallel lines meet. I am my own séance. A happy, better person because a man was kind to me when I was a lesser version of myself, and now he is no longer here.

The school held a celebration of life for him in the high-school gymnasium. He had been a teacher there for just under twenty years, almost half his life. It was standing-room only. An alumnus played a piano solo of one of his favourite songs, Stephen Sondheim's 'Send in the Clowns'.

Everyone cried. It started as a scatter, then spread like a wave. A man doubled over, silently shaking, while a woman rubbed his shoulders. Someone young standing in the back cupped their face, hiding their eyes behind their hand. Someone I might have known sat two rows in front of me, openly weeping. Above the pianist, in one corner of the gymnasium, were the lyrics to our alma mater. Just reading the words brought the melody to my head. Part of Jean Sibelius's 'Finlandia'. I could suddenly remember the opening brass lines. I could picture him conducting it – his long arms, his red hair, the sweeping motion of his hands. Moving with a purpose.

ADAGIO

He was the only thing that could get me to come back to that campus. A single good memory in a place that felt too difficult to remember.

'Pity the Meat': Notes on Iggy Pop

Brian Dillon

Every second he spends on a stage is pregnant still with the possibility he will leave it and join us in the dark. Every performance thus haunted by the vision of a young man risking this adventure for the first time: the first time, as he put it in a 1982 interview with David Letterman, that Iggy *crossed the proscenium*. In the telling, this image – a dream of union with the crowd, a leap out of his own flesh – can be reduced to comedy. Iggy spots in the audience at an early gig two young women lying on the floor looking up at him, and he wonders if they'd like some company, so he jumps off the stage – and the girls roll out of his way. But the extant footage of Iggy going into the crowd is both more noble and more absurd. It is 1970, and the Cincinnati Pop Festival includes Traffic, Alice Cooper, Mountain, Grand Funk Railroad – and the Stooges. With interludes featuring stoned attendees and indulgent Ohio parents, the festival is televised, and a few minutes of the Stooges' set are broadcast. The veteran TV presenter (and former war correspondent) Jack Lescoulie treats proceedings as if he's commentating on a sports event. *There goes Iggy, right into the crowd.*

He is shirtless in blue jeans, a red or brown dog collar at his neck, and a pair of long silver gloves. In the audience, a girl with glasses is drawing a picture of him. The band is in the latter reaches of 'TV Eye', which at a certain point devolves into a one-chord throb during which, to this day, Iggy may get up to anything at all. (Thirty-five years later, with the reunited Stooges, he uses the same interlude to address the front row: *I ain't done with you yet.*) In 1970 he slides down the mic stand, over the lip of the stage, and disappears. Cut to commercials. When Lescoulie returns it's to say that while the show was off-air Iggy has been in and out of the crowd three times. *They seem to be enjoying it, and so does he.* The very striking thing about this footage of a legendarily truculent band and uncontrolled frontman: the Ohio audience seems entirely on his side, willing him on to feats of – what? In this case, not self-destruction but an athletic overcoming of rock's conventional postures, which were already fixed and familiar by the end of the 1960s. Iggy sings a whole verse of '1970' while submerged in the throng. He feels alright! A girl looks up at the roving TV camera: *Please, take a picture, please!* And suddenly Iggy is on his feet, leaps once and fails, tries again and is borne aloft by a dozen hands. *O, I'll leap up to my God! – Who pulls me down?* Iggy is now standing on top of the crowd. A new camera angle, and you can see how it's done: one leg in advance of the other, hands from below tight on his ankles and calves. He raises one silver arm and points – at who?

If you haven't seen the TV footage, you may well know the photograph, taken by Detroit press photographer Tom Copi: Iggy statuesque above the throng, at the apex of an offstage adventure that lasted only forty seconds. (A few years later Bowie, in thrall to the Iggy mythos, would try the same thing and tumble to earth, the crowd insufficiently taken with his Icarus act.) What is he thinking, at this brief and perilous summit? Is his pointing an act of aggression or inclusion? In Copi's photograph, a blonde girl is raised on someone's shoulders – she might be the one seen sketching Iggy in the TV footage. But he seems to point past her. All around, nothing but joy at his daring, surely also at the clownishness of it: like something Buster Keaton or Harold Lloyd might have essayed in a silent short. Beneath him and to his left, someone – someone who may or may not have been thinking of a mock-scatological denouement – hands Iggy a large jar of peanut butter, which he begins scooping out, smearing on his bare chest and flinging into the crowd. According to Copi, when he left the stage later, Iggy wiped what was left of the peanut butter on the shirt of the concert emcee.

Mid-seventies LA: the Stooges are down on their luck and then over. Iggy tries to revive his fortunes, eke out his notoriety, or simply finance his heroin habit, through swiftly botched collaborations with Todd Rundgren and Ray Manzarek of the Doors, then a theatrically sordid show at Rodney's English Disco, where he lies on the floor and is whipped with a chain by Stooges guitarist Ron Asheton, who is dressed as a Nazi. One night, Iggy narrowly avoids death at the hands of irate and gun-wielding drug dealers – they recognise him and decide not to shoot. Around this time, he is frequently picked up by the police, wandering alone or lying comatose outside random apartments. On some of these occasions, Iggy is wearing a dress. In 2011, he would be photographed for the *New York Times* wearing a sleek black cocktail dress and toting a snakeskin Dior handbag. *I'm not ashamed to 'dress like a woman' because I don't think it's shameful to be a woman.*

In 1961 the American photographer William Klein captured an extraordinary 'dance happening' on the streets of Tokyo by three Japanese male Butoh dancers. Two angular, tortured bodies, near-naked; the third in white makeup and a gauzy dress, face and body filled with pathos, is the legendary dancer Kazuo Ohno. Who knows if Iggy had ever seen Klein's picture, or if he was aware – perhaps via Bowie, who borrowed from Butoh – of the surreal rigours of this form of dance. But in a 1979 appearance on the BBC's *Old Grey Whistle Test*, Iggy is all three of Klein's dancers at once, his formerly violent movements now slowed and stylised to a super-confident array of gestures and attitudes. *Forever a dog!* As always, he wrestles with the mic stand as if the two of them are trying to fight or dance in the middle of a crowd. Shirtless in blue cummerbund and tight pants, wide-eyed in mascara, he regards the audience-free studio sternly and flings his arms above his head, does his dislocated-hip dance, forces himself to the floor in a tight bundle of limbs, from which a single arm jerks vertically at the end of 'I Wanna Be Your Dog'. In the last decade of a commercially disastrous career, he has faced down a crowd of Hell's Angels and been badly beaten, poured hot wax on himself (it cools and hardens on the skin, he notes), received oral sex from an audience member of indeterminate gender, flung himself from the stage and onto a table at Max's Kansas City and gouged his flesh on broken cocktail glasses. The question of whether all of this is deliberate is interesting up to a point.

'PITY THE MEAT'

On the 12th of December 1988, Iggy played the National Stadium in Dublin – perhaps an old boxing venue was the aptest forum for his triumphant return bout. He was forty-one and ought to have been punch-drunk or polite, but raged in a way that (aged nineteen) I could not have imagined middle age might contain. 'It's better music than you realise,' he drawled at an uptight TV audience some weeks before. At the Stadium, my friend burst into tears during 'The Passenger'. Others were at the front: *Iggy Pop gave me five!* What had we witnessed? Among other things, some version of a violent maleness without a hint of macho paranoia.

*

Who or what else does he remind me of? Vaslav Nijinsky in 1912 in *L'Après-midi d'un faune*, at once erotic and abstracted or flat, his arms bent stiffly as if he lives in a classical frieze. The Edwardian dancer Maud Allan, shocking first Vienna and then the world in the nearly bare-breasted role of Salome. Charlotte Moorman, the 'topless cellist', interpreter of John Cage and collaborator with Nam June Paik, who Iggy knew all about in avant-garde-friendly Ann Arbor. The Silver Surfer, who first appeared in Marvel Comics in 1966, when Iggy was still drumming for his first band the Prime Movers. (Fred Smith, guitarist with the Stooges' friends the MC5, took the superhero aesthetic more literally, and in the last desperate years of the band's career would appear on stage in his 'Sonic Silver' suit and cape.) Mickey Rooney as Puck in Max Reinhardt's 1935 film of *A Midsummer Night's Dream* – a bowl-cut imp and all-American kid, supernatural agent of desire and confusion. At times Iggy is all of these, an innocent but seductive sprite, a *neighbourhood threat*, a being in flight. (The most recent iteration of his particular energy is not some scuzzily nostalgic and knowing rock'n'roll clown but the shapeshifting, sometimes shirtless Christine and the Queens, also known recently as Redcar or Chris.) In July 1972, the Stooges played their only British concert – that is, until the band implausibly reconvened in 2003 – at King's Cross Cinema in London. The concert was not filmed, but in photographs of Iggy's glittering face and body make-up, his black lips and silver leather trousers, he looks like a human blade. (A year later Martin Amis, who understood nothing about such fascinations, referred to Bowie's 'dinky weapon of a torso' and the 'modish violence' attached to the Ziggy Stardust persona – one assumes Amis had never seen the original of Bowie's leper messiah.) A body made of light, made of energy, such as the choreographer Loie Fuller imagined around 1905 when she danced her dance of radium. In the house they shared in Michigan in the late 1960s, the Stooges would do anything to get high, including in Iggy's case giving himself moderate electric shocks. In certain photographs from the King's Cross gig, he is a walking bolt of lightning.

His is also, that's to say, a body in pain. At times he resembles the flayed man or *écorché* whose skin hangs limp beside him on the page of a medical treatise, while he demonstrates the workings of muscle and sinew – he lives with no borders, no protection. All is visible, and everything strains, like the statue of Laocoön or Frederic Leighton's kitsch Victorian sculpture, *An Athlete Wrestling with a Python*. In 1977, in a piece subtitled 'Blowtorch in Bondage', the rock critic Lester Bangs wrote about Iggy: 'Yeah, Iggy's got a fantastic body; it's so fantastic he's crying in every nerve to explode out of it into some unimaginable freedom.' Bangs, who had championed the Stooges from the start, disparages a recent British journalist's overheated description of Iggy's physical presence. The singer, according to this writer, was 'a hyper-active packet of muscle and sinew, straight out of Michelangelo's wet dreams', an airborne, clawing creature whose performance 'spells one thing – MEAT'. How, Bangs, wants to know, does this person think the meat feels? 'Or if he thinks it feels at all.'

Nowadays he arrives on stage to the sound of barking dogs and the sparse but swaggering opening bars of 'Five Foot One', from his 1979 album, *New Values*. A perfect two-chord riff, plus horns, and there he is in the shadows, already giving us the finger, already calling us *motherfuckers*, which it seems is what we want from him in his seventy-seventh year. He's got a pain in his heart – not that kind. The first thing you notice is Iggy's limp, the way he drags himself to the microphone, before pulling off his waistcoat and hurling the mic stand to the side of the stage, where a roadie picks it up and is ready with another. The limp was obvious in YouTube clips from the past couple of years. More pronounced, in fact: during some concerts Iggy would retreat regularly to a high stool in the middle of the stage. But even there he could not be stilled, and clawed or punched the air as he sang, summoning the ghosts of gestures from half a century ago, without a hint of the melancholy sham that attends his contemporaries. The second thing you notice: this is assuredly the body of a man nearing eighty, his tanned skin hanging in delicate folds. But every inch energised. He looks old – artful and obscene as ever – and somehow younger than any rock star (that antique category) you will see today. In the weeks before Iggy headlined a small festival in south London in the summer of 2023, I caught myself weeping a little at the sight of him online. The sheer victory of it. At some of these concerts (but not in London) he performed 'Hero' by the 1970s German band Neu! – riding through the city, trying to lose his mind.

Marking Time

Ciaran Carson

The year is 198–, and we, by dint of polyphonic after-hours negotiation, by hooks and crooks of bendy roads and out-of-kilter crosses, past the two immobilised Shell petrol pumps stationed on the mossy forecourt of a disused garage, have arrived at O'Looney's Bar, somewhere in the hinterland of Miltown Malbay. It is hardly recognisable as a building, let alone a bar, from its ivy-overgrown outside: it looks more like a hedge – if 'hedge' means 'to shuffle, be evasive, as in argument' – for O'Looney's status as a bar is open to debate. It is, more likely, 'a public house', in its archaic connotation as 'a house open to the public', where the consumption of alcohol is, ostensibly, an afterthought. Or it is a 'shebeen', from the Irish *séibín*, 'a little mug', diminutive of *séibe*, 'a hole, an orifice; a liquid measure, a mug, a bottle' – Dinneen cites the interesting *i mbéal na séibe*, literally, 'in the mouth of the *séibe*', i.e. 'suddenly', or 'unexpectedly', which seems appropriate to O'Looney's. It is impossible to find the front door in its branchy leafy frame of reference, so we go round the back, which is, after all, the customary mode of entry at this unconstitutional hour of the night or morning. In O'Looney's, buried in illicit time, for time out of mind, the front door has become defunct, embedded like a Sanskrit fossil in the Irish-English tongue, its creaking hinge of language rusted stiff forever.

We knock. We knock again. The back door opens up to this ambiguous gloom we walk into. The floor is earth. The smell is mould and alcohol and earth and smoke of turf and nicotine. Candles gutter in their yellow cataracts of wax. A turf fire glows at one end of the room. There is a makeshift bar at the other. In between are shapes hunched over instruments and tunes and tables. Feet pound the earth floor. I get these bearings gradually, as we have some stumbling time to seat ourselves after taking stock of the bar with its basic choice of bottles: stout and whiskey. I find myself wedged in a three-foot-deep window ledge. Gazing upwards through the rafters as the music becomes a mantra, I scan some isolated stars through the holes in the thatch. It could be 18–, but the Guinness calendar affirms that it is otherwise: it is April 1953. 'You can do what toucan do', the slogan says; 'slogan', from the Irish or Gaelic *sluagh-ghairm*, a battle cry, or, more accurately, the 'outcry of a crowd'.

And like some antiquated battle cry of here and now, the Cooleas start up. The Cooleas are up for the weekend from Cúil Aodha, this tiny Gaeltacht on the Cork and Kerry border, and in Coolea, songs are currency. They sing big *sean-nós* songs. They sing comic songs and songs of repartee. They sing newly made songs on the coming of electricity to Coolea, or the first clock ever brought there, and the same clock was kicked useless for its not keeping time, whatever 'time' was back then. They stand their ground in a polyphonic circle in the middle of the floor, holding hands and shoulders as the grain of each voice vibrates against the others and illuminates the others, and their thrown shadows grow enormous on the bumpy pockmarked whitewashed wall and mingle with our shadows. The candles sway and loom, the earthen floor goes 'om', the whole room pulses like a bellows, and the turf fire flares up suddenly to throw the rapt attentive faces of the listeners into chiaroscuro.

They are not an audience, for 'audience' implies a passive formality, and most of these listeners will do something before the night is out: they will sing themselves, or play or dance or tell a yarn or 'rec-imitation', or keep time to the music by a rhythmic rattle of the loose change in their trouser-pockets. Some non-musicians will have the knack of knowing tunes through and through – perfect listeners, for whom it is a joy to play – and, as founts of polyonymous nomenclature, will be ready to supply a name, or several, to the tune known to its player as 'the one after the one that goes before it'. Or some guitar player, oblivious to protocol, after footering and tuning, will start up a three-chord accompaniment in the wrong key in the middle of someone's unaccompanied song. Someone else will comment on the player's marvellous 'accomplishment'.

This is not an audience, but a gathering which invents its programme as it goes along, navigating through the night by dint of many pilots. And the lulls are purposeful, asterisks in time which point eight different ways, like the eight bars of a reel with all its variations. Contracts are made within these temporal nodes; the room becomes an internet. Through the portal of O'Looney's we glimpse the starry fragments of a great galactic internet which shimmers over all the shebeens of the earth – in Ballyvourney or in Boston, in Sydney or in Springfield, Massachusetts, wherever gatherings like this take place and make their sidereal observations. Across the many time zones the same tune might be bi-located at the same time, in the same time.

Layers of cigarette smoke, blue as a Gitanes or Disque Bleu packet, vacillate through the room like microcosmic wavebands. Their frequencies are sputtering and crackling as they're assailed by atmospheric interference and black noise leaks out from the cracks between the lighted station blips. The musicians are like double agents, flitting through the complicated frontiers. They ride the Disque Bleu logo with its wings of Mercury through the Logos of the blue smoke internet and all its shifting laminates. They are subversives of a kind, and they withstand the efforts of officialdom. They will not be regimented, for they are a Maquis, the Second World War Résistance or guerrilla force; *maquis*, from the thicket formation of shrubs on Mediterranean shores, that I imagine is a smoky blue like lavender, shimmering across the scrubby landscape bordering the Raoul Dufy sea. They are not easily uprooted, for their roots are deeply intertangled and form complicated family trees of mutual support. Confederate or Union agents, they blend invisibly across each other's lines, till their blues and greys meet in some other aspect of the spectrum, and another shade of ambiguity is formed. They take each other's versions on and learn each other's shibboleths; 'shibboleth' from the Hebrew for 'torrent':

> Then Jephthah gathered together all the men of Gilead, and fought with Ephraim: and the men of Gilead smote Ephraim, because they said, Ye Gileadites are fugitives of Ephraim among the Ephraimites, and among the Manassites.
>
> And the Gileadites took the passages of Jordan before the Ephraimites: and it was so, that when those Ephraimites which were escaped said, Let me go over; that the men of Gilead said unto him, Art thou an Ephraimite? If he said, Nay;

> Then said they unto him, Say now Shibboleth: and he said Sibboleth: for he could not frame to pronounce it right. Then they took him and slew him at the passages of Jordan: and there fell at that time of the Ephraimites forty and two thousand.
>
> Judges XII, 4–6

Musicians learn to get their tongues round things. They are chameleons, and have independent eyes by which they recognise each other while they blink at someone else. They understand that time itself is a chameleon, so they mark it and they keep it, and they syncopate it. Creatures of a changing blue lagoon, they drift down through its depths like shoals of semiquavers, making new tunes as they swim in temporal agreement.

By this time, dawn is tumultuous in O'Looney's, one singer raising his voice against the chorus of progressively waking birds; the window slowly transforms indigo to sapphire. Then we stumble out into a vast sky opening up before us in a panoply of pink and blue and gold and purple flocks, the bleating of innumerable sheep.

O'Looney's is one of those subjunctive venues where musicianers evade the *hoi polloi* of the designated festival or *fleadh* town. Established by anecdote and shibboleth, they are arrived at by elaborate routines; false trails are laid and misdirections given out. In the town itself, there is a complex ranking of the various pubs, according to their suitability for music and their owners' sense of protocol. Once an equilibrium of musicianers and public is established, the wise owner locks his doors to all those who have not been hitherto inmated. The foolish owner's eyes light up with dollar signs: accessible to all and sundry, his bar is inundated and the music swamped; his returns diminish rapidly, as the music goes elsewhere.

Finding the right bar is a game of chance and skill suitable for x amount of players, and the rules are phrased in a future conditional tense. Clever punters (members of the listening public) will stake out salient pubs and observe the ratio of instrument cases being carried in, then make their move. A cohort of runners will impart the information to the other members of this pact of punters. Meanwhile, musicians leave false scents, like wearing L'Air du Temps instead of Brut; there is an undercover *noir* to everything, as everyone is shadowed. Demographic shifts are made, as many people throng and filter through each other in the street in search of nodes and modes of entertainment and the craic. Paths cross many times and the whole town is a layered chart of footprints.

You cruise the town until the cruise becomes a trawl and possibilities are narrowed down: it's like eating out in London's Soho, where you peruse the menus of a hundred eating houses and it's pot luck whether you eat well or not. You pass the same enticing restaurant so many times that you eventually succumb to its temptation; or, completely spoiled for choice, you are gastronomically confused, and end up with the wrong choice. There are no guarantees, for even the best of places have their off-nights. Trying to allow for all the possibilities, you will be circumvented by the circumstances. So, while there might be some general agreement as to the quality of a *fleadh*, there might be general confusion: one person's *fleadh* is not another's, and not everyone can be in the right place at the right time.

As the town is saturated, movement becomes difficult. It is not unknown for a rake of musicians to play, drink, eat, talk and sleep in the same establishment for four days; and knowing when to stay put requires some art or wisdom. You have to know how to make the best of what there is, and settle for it; and the supposition of a better time elsewhere is mere illusion. Getting there, you have to tune in to the different frequencies of time as your antennae pick up sonic blips and bleeps and the static comes through like the gargled blue noise of locomotive whistles. There are dialects of moods, décors, atmospheres and ambiances. You can fall through trapdoors.

Some unscrupulous publicans, for instance, will put out the word that they have opened up this well-appointed backroom or annex which will extend well after hours, and lure the music in with promises of hospitality. Then when you arrive, you find you are transformed into performing monkeys. There is a cover charge for eager tourists, and there is no escape for you because it's after hours. You are effectively imprisoned: if 'animalcatraz' is US slang for 'zoo' then this place is a 'ceolcatraz'.

Or you find the ideal quiet pub with gorgeous wooden floors and fixtures mirrored in its antique trade mirrors, and you imbibe its atmosphere until you realise that the eccentric owner has forbidden music. He wants his usual clientèle and schedule – 'schedule', from the Latin diminutive of *scheda*, 'a strip of papyrus', something like a bar tab or a check-out print-out with its serried hieroglyphs and computations, marking time and money. He does not want to have his everyday disturbed. He values normal custom. His venue is a discreet forum for the savouring of modicums of talk and alcohol. Jorums are poured as conversations hush around them. A cigarette is lit; a tiny hiss. Ash falls to the quiet floor. And you leave feeling some respect, because there always should be room for this; you realise your status as an interloper.

By this time all the other bars you sussed out hours ago have been packed, so you end up playing in the disused bus station where dogs scavenge for left-overs in the greasy drift of discarded fish and chip and sausage wrappings. Someone has procured a Judas (from 'Iscariot' – 's carry-out) and it's passed around while two drunks shape up for a fight, take a swing at one another and fall down to snore beside each other.

Similarly, you get to know the various dimensions of window-ledges round the town, where three or four musicianers can wedge themselves and set up an impromptu session. Punters gather in a semi-circle, till from the street the players are invisible;

and in this respect, I remember how old punters would perch their antiquated ghetto blasters on a window ledge and give the crowd the benefit of their prized recordings of the fiddle competition. From beyond the semi-circle, it looks just like a session, to the extent that I once observed an ethnomusicologist holding her Nagra mike above the appreciatively nodding heads, the ears cocked to one side, while she footered with her levels and her headphones.

It's possible that such a tape of a tape resides, once or twice removed, in the hermetic archive of the Ulster Folk and Transport Museum. Not for the first time, I wonder about the coupling of 'folk' and 'transport', and am reminded that here, 'folk' is mostly 'material culture' – cottages, a spade mill, stone walls, a schoolhouse, handlooms, churches, and a water-mill. Of particular interest is a bleach-green look-out post built like a birdwatcher's granite sangar, from which the unseen sentry could observe the linen-rustlers, then step out and boldly sound the early-warning system of his pawl-and-ratchet, whirligig-type rattle. It reminds us that Ulster culture resides more in what you do than what you say or sing or play: O linen-weavers, builders of barns, rope-winders, intricate masons! It is but a short step to the vehicle: O makers of motorbikes and tractors! Builders of the *Belfast* and *Titanic*! Constructors of the Harlandic diesel electric locomotive commissioned by the Buenos Aires Great Southern Railway Company! Perfectors of the four-cylinder, triple-expansion, steam-reciprocating engine!

And as children, we were proudly told that Belfast had the biggest shipyard, rope-walk, linen mill, tobacco-works and match manufactory in the world. Even then, the 'had' was *passé*, but the myth persisted and I felt proud as well – Irish as I was, or am – to be a member of this Empire with its cornucopia full of works and pomps. Then, my father would take us to the old Transport Museum in Witham Street, before the concept 'folk' had been invented. This was a cold dank converted engine-shed or tram-depot. We loved its gloom and smell of oil and iron, the palpable whiff of steam long since expired. Enormous locomotives loomed above us as we gawped at them open-jawed. We would climb aboard a tram and sit in the open-top deck, and my father would sniff and wipe his eyes because he'd remembered his father taking him on board a tram just like this, and he could feel the wind of time blow in his ears and eyes.

The old Transport Museum persisted a good many years after the establishment of the Ulster Folk and Transport Museum at Cultra,* and I used to bring my own children there and experience that generational shiver. Now, the whole shebang has

---

* Philologically, the Museum is aptly located. A straightforward translation of *cúl trá* might be 'behind the strand' or 'the hinterland of the strand' (cf. Scottish *ahint*, 'behind'); but *trá* as a verb means 'to ebb', and is surely related to *tráth*, 'a period of time; once upon a time; a season' and other time-related concepts. So the place name might be glossed as 'the hinterland of time', or, 'at the back of once upon a time'. *Idir-thráth* is 'twilight'; so we are getting very close to 'the twilight zone'.

been transported, lock, stock and barrel, to Cultra, and housed in a giant glass and concrete hangar. The same enormous locomotives are there, somewhat diminished by the Brobdingnagian ceiling; and the atmosphere is different, for now everything is in a context. Many details have been added to convince us that the past is here and now. There is an authentic newsvendor's kiosk; pockmarked enamel adverts for defunct brands of tea and cigarettes; the cafe is a station replica; period-costumed dummies relax stiffly in their leather-perfumed carriages. In one such thematic figment, a cassette of atmospheric platform noise is broadcast throughout the vast resounding hall: 'All ab-o-o-a-r-rd for Ballymena! Pe-e-e-p, pe-e-p! Whis-s-st. Psssst. Psst. Pst. Po-o-o-o-p, po-o-o-p! Choo-chuh-chuh, choo-chuh, chunk, chuff, chuff chuff. Ticka-tick-a-tick,' till it fades away and leaves behind imaginary puffs of smoke, and a lull of silence as the tape rewinds.

And they have added strange contraptions from the age of narrow-gauge: hybrid locomotive buses; tandem quadricycles; squat black Guinness mules that transported porter through the labyrinthine brewery; mobile donkey-engines from the shipyard; things that look like time-machines in their perfect, cast-iron, antiquated futuristic design, with their milled-brass knobs and thumbscrews, their plate-glassed Captain Nemo dials with steel needles stilled in them.

Everything is analogue, and looks like something else. Everything is *déjà vu*.

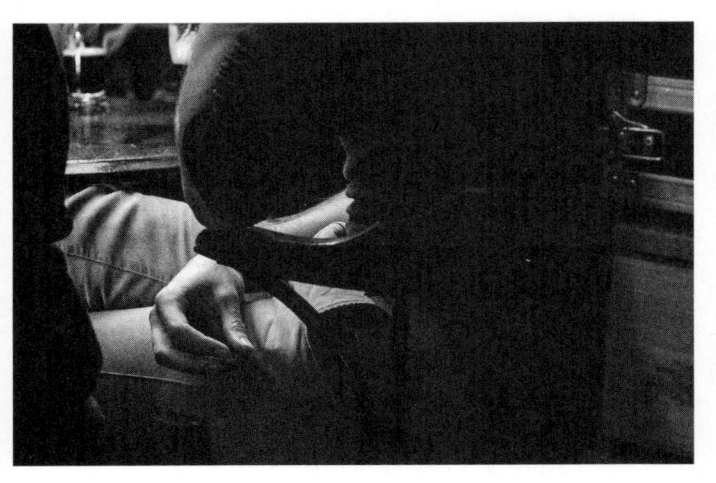

Alien Lanes

Peter Geoghegan

There is a scene in *Almost Famous*, Cameron Crowe's film about a high-school kid in the early '70s who is given the chance to write for *Rolling Stone*, where the lank-haired protagonist meets legendary rock writer Lester Bangs. Sitting in an empty diner, the late afternoon sun streaming through the windows, Bangs, played by the late Philip Seymour Hoffman, warns the cub reporter that 'you cannot make friends with the rock stars'.

Almost Famous is a forgettable movie, but I must have watched it a dozen times after its release. At the time, I was also in my teens and dreaming of becoming a music journalist. I had my own fanzine, *Oral Blessings* (an awful name, I know). It was a mix of reviews of new records and interviews with fictitious bands. I photocopied each issue at the local library and handed it out to mostly nonplussed classmates in my secondary school in Longford, a small town not far from a bog that sits across much of Ireland's central plain.

My teenage dreams were indulged at home. My father bought me a cut-price stereo with a twin cassette deck for my birthday one year. After Sunday mass, my mother would allow me to choose between the *New Musical Express* and *Melody Maker* in the shop beside Longford Cathedral. Most weeks I went for the *NME*.

And all the while, like my role model in *Almost Famous*, I wanted to make friends with the stars. Bjork. Jarvis Cocker. Nick Cave.

But the one rock star I *really* wanted to befriend was never on the covers of the inky music papers. It was only years later that I learned that at the time Robert Pollard, lead singer of Guided by Voices, was struggling to scrape a living, having not long given up his job as an elementary-school teacher in his hometown of Dayton, Ohio. I was surprised because for me, and a small group of my school friends, Guided by Voices were just about the biggest band in the world. They were certainly the coolest.

Guided by Voices could be the most prolific band in pop music history. Imagine if peak Beatles had lasted decades, not years.

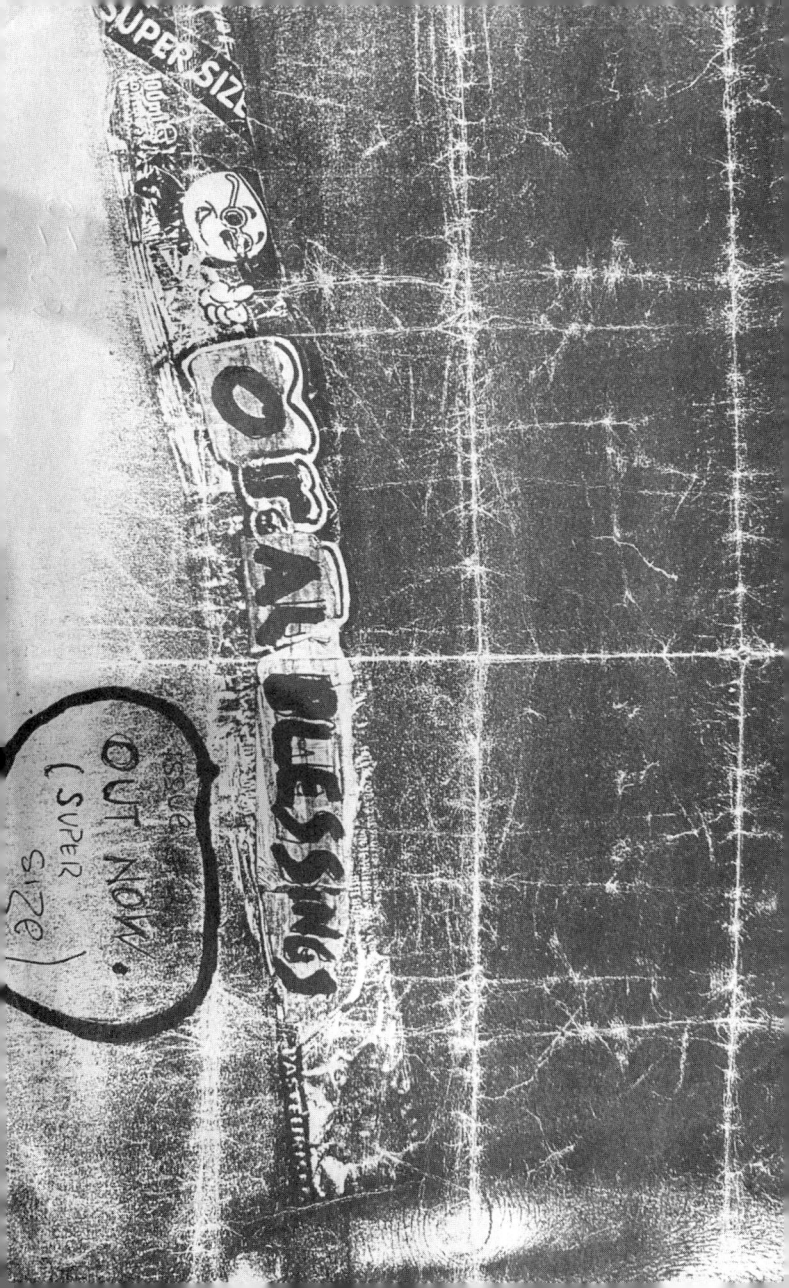

GBV fan forums argue over how many records the band has released. The website *Discogs* counts seventy-nine LPs, plus ninety-one singles and EPs since their 1986 debut. Robert Pollard is listed as having also released thirty-one solo records, alongside myriad side projects and off-cuts. Pollard is said to have a suitcase filled with thousands of songs that he has yet to record.

The one constant in this whirr of productivity is the GBV sound: many of Pollard's best moments sound like they were recorded on a 1980s answering machine. It's lo-fi as lifestyle choice. And it's glorious. Scratchy, jagged garage rock, with scattergun lyrics and glorious pop hooks that burst into flame for two minutes before, often abruptly, segueing into the next sonic assault.

My favourite Guided by Voices album, *Bee Thousand*, was released in 1994. It races through twenty tracks in less than thirty-seven minutes. Where most vocalists sang about love, or drugs, or both, Pollard seems to sing in free association. *Bee Thousand*'s standout tracks have titles such as 'The Goldheart Mountaintop Queen Directory', 'Buzzards and Dreadful Crows', and 'Tractor Rape Chain'. I have no idea what they are about. But since the first time I heard them, I loved them. *We* loved them.

✷

Seamus Heaney has a great line about the mundanity of 1960s Belfast: 'If a coat hanger knocked in a wardrobe/That was a great event.' When I first read those lines, years later when I was working in Belfast, I thought of my own youth.

Rural Ireland in the late 1990s was a place of great change. About thirty miles north from Longford, the Troubles was ending in Northern Ireland. The Republic's economy was on the crest of a boom. Divorce was legalised. Condoms were no longer surreptitiously shipped across the border.

But little of this change, momentous as it was, filtered down into the everyday life of a teenager in a small Irish town. My school was run by Catholic priests. It was single sex, just like every other school in the purlieus. We rote learned an English syllabus that didn't have room for Heaney and his contemporaries but did include Alexander Pope and John Dryden. Our Irish history course stopped in 1968, the year that the civil rights movement started across the border. We were not taught about the civil war that descended soon after.

I can't remember exactly when I was introduced to US indie music, but I would have been around fourteen or fifteen. I think it started when the boy who sat next to me in geography, a rather quiet kid named Andrew, began bringing tapes of the Pixies into school. Andrew had sandy hair and came from a small farming village about ten miles away. The Pixies cassettes belonged to his older brother. I had a Walkman, and Andrew and I would sit down the back of class, an ear each, listening to the tinny sound of *Surfer Rosa* and *Bossanova* while Mr. McGuiney delivered sermons on oxbow lakes and U-shaped valleys. (Our mischief was more daring than it sounds: despite a ban on corporeal punishment introduced a decade or so earlier, Mr. Guiney was prone to whacking noisy pupils across the head with an open palm.)

My listening sessions with Andrew became a regular fixture in my school week. Once we had finished the Pixies, he brought in more of his brother's collection: the Breeders, Pavement, Mudhoney. After much pleading, Andrew allowed me to borrow the tapes – one at a time – so I could record them at home. These pirated cassettes I traded, mainly with a group of about ten or twelve schoolmates who liked the same bands.

Music was not the only thing we had in common. We didn't play Gaelic football – the sport that was our school's only real claim to fame – and most of us lived in the town, rather than among the endless perpendicular fields of County Longford. We aped the grunge culture we saw on *My So-Called Life*, differentiating ourselves from the 'jocks' by growing our hair long and wearing oversized T-shirts.

We scrawled the names of our favourite bands in Tipp-Ex on schoolbags that we uniformly slung across one shoulder. (Teenage rules can often be as arbitrary as they are iron.) A couple of the bands were British, but even those had a distinctly American sound: My Bloody Valentine, The Wedding Present. But otherwise, all the names were US, and often the most prominent space was reserved for one outfit: Guided by Voices.

We knew GBV were cool, which was probably a big part of why we liked them so much. The two fusty record shops in town didn't sell their records; we had to wait for a trip to Dublin to buy them. In the meantime, we would swap copies of the GBV cassettes we did have and sit up late on Sunday nights to record their songs off the only radio show we knew that played 'our music', a show called *Alternative Cuts* that ran on the local FM radio station.

The DJ on *Alternative Cuts* was a laconic guy who went by the nickname 'Gonzo'. He was a few years older than us. At the time, I thought it was the best job in the world. It was only later that I learned that a couple of hours a week in the graveyard slot – before an automated feed of country music kicked in – was more vocation than profession. My friends and I would often ring in with requests, peppered with cryptic references to recent events in our small world. I once made the mistake of asking for a derivative Britpop record. Gonzo was not impressed. 'That's not real music.'

We didn't just listen to our heroes, we tried to imitate them. We formed bands that played covers of Pavement, GBV, and the like. Occasionally these bands would swap the garage for a draughty parish hall, where a dozen lads would try to pogo while a singer affected an American accent, and a rhythm section bludgeoned its way through another indie pop song. A few of the bands did go on to write their own material – some of which I 'released' on cassettes sellotaped to later iterations of my fanzine – but most broke up long before then.

A few years later, Guided by Voices announced that they were playing a show in Dublin. I was in university on the west coast by then, but was still close to my school friends. We all bought tickets for the show the day they were released. Our alacrity was unnecessary: the show was far from sold out. At least half the crowd seemed to be from Longford. I met people I hadn't seen since secondary school, crowd-surfing down the front.

If the meagre attendance bothered Robert Pollard, it didn't show. He bounced around the stage. He drank beer prodigiously in the breaks between songs. The band closed the show with a cover of the Beatles' 'A Hard Day's Night'. As Pollard walked off stage, he looked as pleased as we were.

So why did a clutch of US indie bands hold such attraction for a bunch of awkward teenagers in rural Ireland? In one sense it's obvious. Many of us were adopting the interests and studied poses of older siblings or the cool kids a few years our senior. But even then, why were *they* so drawn to these bands? Perhaps it's because there was some similarity between the worlds these bands emerged from – often driven, like us, by booze and boredom – and the world we were growing up in.

Some of the most influential US indie outfits emerged in cities and towns far from the progressive coasts. Hüsker Dü and the Replacements came out of

Minneapolis and St Paul. Wilco formed in Chicago. The Breeders, the Afghan Whigs, and Guided by Voices all come from Ohio. Like Longford, this is 'flyover country', places often forgotten about, if they were ever remembered in the first place.

A decade after my first fanzine, I did become a journalist. Unlike the greenhorn reporter in *Almost Famous*, I have never written for *Rolling Stone*, but I did get a chance to visit Guided-by-Voices country when I drove across the Midwest in 2016 to cover the presidential campaign that would end with Donald Trump in the White House.

I travelled with an old friend who was moonlighting as my cameraman. One of our first stops was Youngstown, Ohio. Like GBV's hometown of Dayton, Youngstown is a solidly blue-collar city. It once boasted twenty-five miles of steel mills. They're now abandoned, and Youngstown is best known for the titular track by Bruce Springsteen. The evening we arrived, I got food poisoning in the Japanese restaurant on the other side of the eight-lane highway that sat in front of our motel. I spent most of the next day reporting from a rehab centre for opioid addicts. Ohio has one of the highest levels of drug deaths in the US.

A few years earlier, I had become, briefly, a bête noire for local politicians in Longford after I wrote a long piece for an Irish newspaper about the influx of heroin into my hometown. One town councillor asked during a council meeting if I 'could not have written about Athlone' – the nearest large town – 'instead'.

As we drove through the flat plains of central Ohio talking to voters, I often found myself thinking of home. Longford had a tough '80s, too. It never had the scale of the Midwest's heavy industry – or the well-paid blue-collar jobs that went with it – but one of my earliest political memories is of pickets outside a factory in Longford town. It was 1988. The owner of a local factory that fitted out ambulances wanted to downsize. His workers went on strike. After months of industrial action, the boss closed the factory down and moved the business to South Africa. More than three decades later, Longford has never really recovered.

Guided By Voices went on to become bona fide, if unlikely, rock stars. The Strokes seem to namecheck GBV in almost every interview. Steven Soderbergh wrote the foreword to one of numerous books about GBV. The band's sound remained defiantly lo-fi, but the records were no longer recorded in carports and basements in Dayton and were sold around the world.

Success brought friction, too: the original GBV line-up reformed in 2010, but split in acrimony three years later. The last time I saw GBV, in a small London club not long before the pandemic, it was Robert Pollard and a cast of session musicians. I didn't much care, to be honest. One of my oldest friends from Longford pretended to be sick so he could get the day off work to come. The band played for almost three hours. Pollard, now in his sixties, screamed until he was hoarse. I lost count of how many cans of beer he drank.

The set ended with the Who's 'Baba O'Riley'. We stumbled out into London's night air with its chorus of 'Teenage Wasteland' ringing in our ears.

Visions of Johanna

M. John Harrison

The only thing I know about music is that it has excited me since I first heard Bill Haley & His Comets do 'Rock Around the Clock'. In 1956, product like that brought me automatically into collision with my father's preferences. He liked Chopin. He liked Beethoven. He liked Maria Callas and Kathleen Ferrier. He loved 'Die Fledermaus', and he played it to us, his family, a lot. When I played him Lonnie Donegan in return, or allowed myself to be discovered flailing around the front room to Elvis Presley's 'Heartbreak Hotel', he lost his temper almost immediately. A tone was set between us.

The only tune we had in common was a muted, alchemical reappraisal of 'Moonlight in Vermont' by the Gerry Mulligan Quartet. This played itself out in three or four minutes on a 78rpm single, and my father and I were forced to enjoy it separately, because it was clear we were receiving widely different communications. He liked 'Moonlight in Vermont' because it was clever but not too clever. I liked it because it put me into a curiously passive mood I didn't understand, a condition that – in combination with and opposition to the raw intensity of tunes like 'Rock Around the Clock' – helped define and steer my relationship with every kind of art from then on. I don't like to know why I like what I like: but I can't let anything go until I've engaged and re-engaged and finally owned it. Owning is better than understanding.

That's the use of music.

My father died in 1958. We were never able to build out from Mulligan's mood piece, or find any way of using it as a bridge. By then, anyway, my ear was nailed every night to my transistor, and the uneasy listening that was Radio Luxembourg – an activity more like receiving secret messages in occupied France in 1943 than hearing music. 208 metres, medium wave: night after night, more atmospherics than signal, more interference than popular song. The effort to transcribe a complete verse, let alone make sense of it, became less entertainment than moral commitment. It was tiring. It was beamed in from another planet. I knew I didn't want 'Itsy Bitsy Teenie Weenie Yellow Polka Dot Bikini'. But what did

I want? Tipping point followed tipping point. Chuck Berry toppled me over into Bo Diddley and thence into Howlin' Wolf. I had already begun to borrow the blues albums of my friends; I hadn't dared admit to – let alone play for the dead father – any of those.

1963, all confusion was brought to a close. Alone in the house, I watched *The Madhouse on Castle Street*, a BBC TV drama throughout which a young, intense, American white man with a weird, raw-looking shock of hair sat at the bottom of some stairs in what was supposed to be a British suburban home and played a guitar and sang. He was small like me. He was equally angry. He had nothing to do with the fiction he was in – that we were all in – and he was aching with the news of that. He had no contribution but to appear as who he was, a trick I would still be trying to master fifty years later. *The Madhouse on Castle Street* wasn't much good, though the making of it was a madhouse in itself, and its history is worth looking up on YouTube. But everything went out the window for me with the appearance of that raw ageing boy, the early Bob Dylan, and nothing was ever going to be the same again. Whoever – whatever – I listened to or read or watched subsequently would be measured against him.

Everyone knows what happens to Dylan around 1964. He becomes difficult to parse. The plain, old-fashioned rhetoric is traded in for symbols more internalised, adventures more personal and sinister. Lines bizarre yet disturbingly from life, transition between the heartfelt and the hermeneutic. He burns his bridges in every image, every line of the verse, relying on charisma and the romance of himself to carry him into the chorus. The shift from a social, almost localised politics into concerns of personality, identity, alienation, and metaphysics isn't sudden. That which is being mourned, castigated, or celebrated develops almost methodically, from *Another Side of Bob Dylan*, through *Bringing It All Back Home* to *Highway 61 Revisited* and its completion as a trajectory in the masterwork of *Blonde on Blonde*. What he loses is the bleak folksiness. What he doesn't lose is a certain brutality of vision. His tone is still accusatory: I see you. Only it's harder to say who or what he sees, exactly; especially when it's himself he's looking at.

What is being mourned or celebrated in the 'Visions of Johanna'? I don't know. Who was Johanna, in the real life of the writer? Back then it was harder to find out than it would be now. I soon discovered I didn't care: biography is fun, gossip is fun, but neither of them are what anything is about, and the facts are no explanation of anything. Living without Wikipedia, a twenty-year-old escapee from the Midlands of the UK, I received Johanna not as an *à clef* but as a world. At that time, everywhere had become a kind of Radio Luxembourg of its own: fragmented, blitzed by static, undependable of wavelength, crammed into a bandwidth too narrow to tell the whole story, transmitted from some station out there I didn't know, in ways I didn't understand. These visions were a communication directly from the heart of it. By *Blonde on Blonde*, I wasn't even sure what Dylan was complaining about, except that it wasn't anything as simple or easily presented – anything as outgoing – as nuclear disarmament.

I only knew that when he sang in that way, or looked at the camera like that, he was me; but that, crucially, I could never be him.

A note on singing. Dylan is almost never singing. He is having an attitude, conveyed as much by some kind of impatient body language as by words. Equally he does not play music, or compose poetry. All his language, you feel, implies, or stands in for some other language or combination of languages, and what he means is written in, or somehow emerges from that combination. It's invisible yet unmistakable, gloriously loud and absolutely unforgiving: I'm not sure I would have given him a Nobel Prize, because I don't think they give one for that.

So what's the narrative here? A man who might or might not have a place in the fiction awaits a woman called Johanna. While it's hard to care who she was in Bob Dylan's real life, I've often imagined her as the woman in the red pants suit on the front of the earlier album *Bringing It All Back Home*. Some days I see her as the Joan Didion immortalised in Julian Wasser's portraits a year or two later. Sue me. Anyway, it's night. The heat pipes are noisy. Rail yards are close enough to be heard. The rain falls like a metaphor. In the loft there's our narrator and a woman called Louise, and Louise's lover. There are others, but they are not named, though they are described at what is – given the briefness of a song – length. Like many of Dylan's characters at that time, they're a roster of the offences they've committed against him. Louise has no real existence, for instance, except inasmuch as she is not Johanna. Although not being Johanna – and being a disappointment for that – is her major characteristic, other qualities are inferred. She's 'all right', she's 'just near'. It's damning. In the end nothing happens, nothing is told, although many things have been noticed and reviewed; we have been allowed into the museum and seen some fragments of what's on display. The fiddler's account has been settled. In the end there have been more people in here than we thought, and they have passed through, and clearly Johanna, like Godot, isn't going to arrive. By then the backing-track sounds a bit mousy and distant, as if some of the instruments are playing in another building. Fake farm-boy harmonica wails across it like the real, unforgiving narrative that has all this time been needing to be heard. It is, in short, a vibe.

These days I listen obsessively to William Basinski's 'Disintegration Loops'. Also, the degraded ballroom fragments of Leyland Kirby, supposed to mimic the condition of Alzheimer sufferers – a group that, statistically, I can have reasonable expectations of joining quite soon. I'm as keen to keep going as I always have been, as if energetic movement forward in time will somehow protect me from the very event I'm trying to avoid. Once or twice a year, though, I return to these images of Johanna and let their ethic of jangling acid romance and transcendental male narcissism wash me into the late '60s version of myself, in the innocent and absolutely pure knowledge that my father would have hated the loft, the rain, Bob Dylan, Johanna, and, especially, the fish truck unloading in the NY dawn. Every three or four listens, I ask myself: what if it's actually Louise who would have looked like Joan Didion posing so awkwardly in front of her Corvette Stingray in 1968?

The Last Place that Felt like Home

Sydney Weinberg

When I was a kid growing up in the suburbs of Atlanta, a clock radio woke me each school day at 6 a.m. Sometimes it was the DJ's ragged laugh that hustled me out of dreamland, but more often it was the tail-end of some overplayed nineties pop song: until recently, I would've said 'Tubthumping' or 'My Heart Will Go On'. Every six months or so, I would accidentally knock the radio to the floor, or a power outage would strike, and the morning show to which I'd become accustomed would vanish into static, and I would be obliged to navigate through a frantic grey sea of sound to a new morning show. In the days and weeks following this abrupt shipwrecking, I would wake disoriented, missing the familiar DJ pair who bickered in a flirtatious but family-friendly way and were probably younger than I am now. Slowly, I would adjust to a new set of hosts, who'd bicker in a similar way and play the same songs, and then I'd mess up the dial again somehow and the discombobulation would repeat. There never seemed any sure way to return to a preferred station; it was as though the stations disappeared into the ether whenever I lost them, and could only be recovered by chance.

When I was fourteen and my sister was eleven, our family moved to Panama, and all those songs that had played faintly in the background as we brushed our teeth or rode shotgun to sleepovers dissipated into the ether for good. In Panama, an entirely different roster of Spanish-language songs dominated the airwaves. At the time, I didn't notice or mind: I'd never before thought about whether or not I liked the songs playing on my clock radio. They were chosen for me, the same way a beribboned dress for Passover or broccoli casserole for dinner was chosen for me. By the time I was old enough for college, the internet had made available a vast catalogue of music that transcended space and time. Choice was suddenly lavishly available. As it did for so many others, music became for me a means of self-expression. In the decades since the American part of my childhood was severed, I've returned to the US only in brief stints. The more ubiquitous of those old radio songs have manifested on far-flung ironic dancefloors since, but many others – the sad, uncool ballads – vanished forever into the static I used to field with my dial, as did the stations, the interchangeable DJs, the girl I was, the person I thought I would become.

I live in London now, where one languid and innocuous Sunday morning I stayed in bed drinking ceremonial cacao and following an internet rabbit hole to its endpoint on Spotify. A song title caught my eye: 'Breathe (2 AM)', by Anna Nalick. It seemed familiar, but I couldn't say why: I didn't recognise the singer's name, nor could I summon the melody. When I clicked play, however, a song I knew by heart flowed through me like a paralytic medicine. I listened to the song in its entirety and when it finished, I selected 'Go to song radio'. This was a function I used often to find new artists and generate playlists according to mood, but clicking it now automatically unearthed a sonic time capsule. Here was song after song rescued from the static and resplendent with cathartic car rides; windows reached only by diligent climbers; cataclysmic kisses on empty football fields; dead-end jobs, alcoholic lovers, and hard-won sagacity. Almost all the songs were by female singer-songwriters, headliners from the heyday of Lilith Fair or else categorically adjacent (there was very little Tori Amos, Aimee Mann, and certainly no Ani DiFranco getting played), describing the joys but more commonly the disappointments of womanhood. It is, retrospectively, a counterintuitive soundtrack for the era in which most adults were busy telling girls we could be anything we wanted to be. By contrast, most of these songs were offering fatalistic preparations for the future. There had been, for me, a certain glamour to the warning: my parents were miserable together, and I would've rather suffered the consequences of my own misguided adventures.

I know all this because mummified inside each song was the truncated consciousness of the girl I'd been, a girl so altered by transplantation to Panama that she'd become someone else with a new set of skills, fears, and pleasures. The person I became had relinquished, perhaps necessarily, all attachment to the mint-green bedroom with the plastic vines of wisteria draped along the ceiling, the three teddy bears, and the lamp that responded to touch. And the clock radio, of course. In bed with my cacao, I felt like an amnesiac recovering blacked-out fragments of a life.

The second song to make it onto my playlist was Natalie Imbruglia's 'Torn'. This was a song I remembered well and found unprompted. In Georgia, we'd lived in an eccentric hilly neighbourhood – a nature preserve, actually, with strange wooden houses scattered through a forest – and the long yellow school bus dropped us kids at the community swimming pool because the hills were too treacherous to climb.

My sister and I, plus two neighbour girls, dawdled on our way home, licking the stamens of honeysuckles and singing a Pink Floyd mondegreen taught to us by one girl's older brother, a rallying cry against 'educashun' and 'forced control'. That, and 'Torn'. The cognitive dissonance at play in sheltered eleven-year-olds wailing about how it was too late for us, we were torn already, makes me smile and skewers me with strange nostalgia. To have been, back then, so innocent and nerve-racked and compelled by the unknown. Why exactly was the singer bound and broken on the floor? Was it true that illusions never changed into something real? To be torn both physically and emotionally – that much was clear to me – foretold a dark erotic inheritance; the word 'torn' alone had once infused me with a directionless melange of shame and desire.

Another song that conveyed an alluring frisson of mature regrets was Paula Cole's 'I Don't Want to Wait'. It was the theme song to *Dawson's Creek* – a show I wasn't allowed to watch – and it told a story about a sad woman trying not to have too sad a life. It seemed to hint that a duller destiny followed the enchantingly ephemeral one implied by Sixpence None the Richer's silver moon and fireflies in 'Kiss Me'. Listening to Jewel in my London bedroom, I was struck by the demure piety of her lyrics, which nevertheless twisted acrobatically, though the morning's biggest revelation was Natalie Merchant's 'Wonder'. This was one of the songs that failed to spark an iota of recognition before I clicked on it, but hearing the melody was like meeting a sibling I'd forgotten I had. The intimate cadence of the opening, the way she sang the words 'no explanation': there was magic to it. Instead of predicting the future, these songs now snowglobed the past.

Perhaps my favourite recovered song was 'Fast Car', Tracy Chapman's hypnotic dirge about a woman who can't seem to lift herself out of poverty, who dreams vividly of escape. The song charts the death of her hope and features as a choral motif the eponymous fast car, driven by a lover who won't make good. In rediscovering this song, I was obliged to recognise that I have felt, all my life, an enduring gothic attraction to Chapman's heroine's dilemma: stay and accept a static, unfulfilling, possibly abusive existence, or leave, and in doing so, pass beyond the pale. It's a desperado's dilemma, arriving at a sublimely lucid and inarguable moment that brooks no delay and can never be undone: squint at that choice and you'll see it glowing through the whole of literature like a spray of germs under ultraviolet light. Charlotte and Harry in Faulkner's *The Wild Palms* make it; Joyce has Eveline face it in *Dubliners*. The choice (and its attendant moment) is present in Henry James, it's in Forster, it's in Jean Rhys. It's often a woman's choice: I'm not surprised to find it resounding so prominently during this era of songwriting. I think I've always been afraid of entrapment, and thus entranced by the choice. I'd felt trapped in Panama, as a teenager: conveyed into the unknown against my will and forced to adapt. When adulthood came (and with it, autonomy), I always got in the fast car. To think that now I was listening to the genesis of that angst. Like a foundational lesson taught in a schoolroom in a dream.

*

Recently, it occurred to me to share the playlist with my sister. I don't know why I didn't think of it before – probably because we have little in common, including taste in music. But the playlist was different, it turned out, because it originated in the era before choice. The schism that the move to Panama occasioned in my life was also detectable in my sister's: she's convinced she was younger than she was when we moved, and her Spanish is perfect, much better than mine. Sometimes she can't find the phrase or word she's looking for in English. She tried to return to the US for college, but wound up dropping out and moving to Korea. She's fluent in Korean, too. She moved back to the US a few years ago, after going on a Tinder date while visiting our mother. If ever I text her reminders of our American childhood – Blue Bell ice-cream sandwiches, Google Earth links to the street we lived on – she responds with indifference, as if I'm bothering her with the trivia of a movie she doesn't particularly remember or like. Georgia is, for me, the last place that ever felt like home, but my sister was in Panama for longer and it became home for her. I didn't have high hopes for her response to the playlist, but she replied the next day:

Still running through the list but so far I had that whoah omg to:

Breathe (2 AM)
Stay (I missed you)
Bitch
Adia
Foolish Games
I'm the Only One

But also some of these songs are worse than I remember? Haha

Then later:

Just hit 10,000 miles and I legit can't listen without crying

Later still:

I told everyone at work about the playlist and they were like why are so many of these songs SO SAD

My sister's favourite playlist find was the weepy and prolific Sarah McLachlan, who like Jewel, had many hits, most memorably the enigmatic 'Adia'. What was she saying? The sound blurred as she sang. *Adiadobelieve I've failed you* ... It was a woman's name, my sister said, but it was also a feeling. I agreed. It seemed like the name for the feeling in which I'd insatiably submerged myself during the days that followed the initial assembly of the playlist: nostalgia for a future that had never materialised. Perhaps this was not symptomatic of the move to Panama; perhaps an entire generation, rocked by the explosive development of tech, endless housing crises, and the apocalyptic spectre of climate change, longs for a future that dissolved upon approach. It wasn't like those radio songs promised us happiness, health, or riches, but they did seem to suggest that a small life was not without dignity. I guess I thought it might not be so bad, growing up to be a sad woman, so long as I was also a wise one. Hardship seemed to me then a privilege of the adulthood I craved; it was practically romantic.

Now, romance is one of memory's tricks. And so the feeling of 'Adia', which once spawned myriad projections of future selves, now webs around the past, describing not who I became but who I once was. Crusty-eyed at 6 a.m. amid the flirtatious bickering of my favourite DJs. Sliced bananas and Honey Nut Cheerios for breakfast. My dad scraping ice from the windshield of his jeep. Finding his Green Card on my mom's desk: a picture of him looking young and wild under the word ALIEN. The long halls, the memorised locker combinations, the teachers bulky in velour. Wandering home from the bus stop, foraging blackberries and pretending I was Sam from *Now and Then* (my sister was Roberta). The screaming fights emanating from neighbours' windows and our parents' bedroom. The squirrels disembowelled by the cats, out on the deck. Swim practice in the summer; the lollipop rings with their reducible jewel; the beloved bus driver – Miz Davis – who died of a stroke; the jumpy miniature greyhound owned by our parents' friends; the Barnes & Noble where I'd be dropped off and left in the children's section to read for hours, as if it were a library. La Madeleine, which was a special treat, where I always had a fruit tart and my sister ordered an éclair. The friends who became enemies and then friends again. The sleepovers where we dressed up in dirndls and watched *Star Wars* and played MASH. The ancient unicycle some neighbourhood kids found in the drained lake and cleared of mud. The stench of dead fish in the sun. Reading in the bushes after school until my mother remembered to collect me. 'Adia' emanating from the car like gas when I got in and didn't bother asking what took her so long. Then the driver's license I never got, the part-time job I never held, the boyfriend I never kissed. When I first rediscovered those songs, I felt returned to the brink of all that – as if I were getting the chance to do it over, become the ghost of old hopes. For weeks, I binged nothing but the playlist, until like an ancient mystic tablet exposed to corrupting air, its sharper inscriptions began to fade.

Good Life

McKenzie Wark

I don't even know which rave it was. We'd gone deep into the morning. Swept under by sound and light, like some aquatic, many-tentacled beast, flailing into the damp and dark. The DJ – who even was it? – dropped an edit of 'Good Life', prompting a tremor of recognition, a tantalising chill of collective joy.

It's always strange to be reminded that this track, so special to me, is not special to me alone. Others have their histories with it. Others have connections in nerve and flesh and memory that unfurl to its signature opening synth sound. 'Good Life', by Inner City, connects me to Sydney, at the end of the eighties. Nights at the Kommotion or the Freezer. Friends still fondly felt who drifted away, or sank.

Something about 'Good Life' felt contemporary, back then. Something about its lack of sonic residue. Its slim reference to analogue-era instruments and to dance music commonplaces. It felt like the sound of the machine itself, and still does. There's something liquid about it, about how it trickles into your body, moves it.

The vocal also seduces. There's none of the pyrotechnics of classic disco-diva voicing. It's intimate, cool. An invitation, an initiation, just for you. It's a song about a longing, a want, a need. To be free, to be free of pain, of anguish. Freedom is the feeling of no fear, as Nina Simone declared. The 'Good Life' vocal isn't particularly hopeful. There's no anger in it, either. It's the voice of the late eighties, a cool and desperate era, long after the scuppering of so many dreams.

Later, I'll learn that the track was made by Kevin Saunderson, one of the architects of Detroit techno. It might be the first techno-adjacent track I ever heard. I'll learn that the vocal was written and performed by Chicago singer Paris Grey. The lyrics always remind me of another track that's special to me: 'Good Times' by Chic. That one still had that late-seventies cresting uplift, in spite of it all. A decade later, with 'Good Life', things had changed.

I had that first album by Inner City, and the 12-inch of 'Good Life'; I'd put them on and dance around the kitchen while doing the washing up. Later I got it on compact disc from a discount bin. Sometimes music sticks like that. Comes forward through time. I'm not usually one for musical nostalgia. I want to hear what the present sounds like. That's the job of pop music: the now-sound. Sometimes the now that a song sounds out ripples on for a long time. 'Good Life' still sounds like now to me.

∗

I emigrated from Sydney to New York in 2000. I'd fallen in love with a New Yorker. I selected one case of compact discs to bring with me and gave the rest away. That Inner City album made the cut. I played it on the long flight across the Pacific Ocean. It sounded clean, cool, and American. It sounded like where I was headed. To the heart of the empire.

Most of what I know about America I learned from Black music. It's the source I trust the most. It's what taught me about the pain and the violence of this restless, relentless land in which I'd live the latter half of my life. It's not my music. It's like I hear it through the wall. I still think it's the greatest art this land of blood and terror ever produced.

'Good Life' sounds out a particular place and time in the American saga, tapping into the empire's *latent* destiny. As DeForrest Brown Jr. argues in *Assembling a Black Counterculture*, techno is the sound of the Black experience in the era of deindustrialisation. A people who moved north, in search of a better life, drawn to the cities and factories of the Midwest and beyond, then thrown back on their own resources as industry picked up and left for elsewhere.

Techno came, not so much from Detroit, as the suburbs outside it. Music made by young Black men feeling the mood around them. Taking up the products of the industrial age, repurposing its music-making machines, making them make music otherwise. It's the sound of a fresh kind of pain – and possibility. How to pick up the pieces from the ruins of modern, industrial life, and make another sound, another sense, with them.

There's a little of New York in this sound, too. The energy of its dance floors. Kevin Saunderson had spent some time there. Who would have expected a straight dude to make such a cute queer anthem? It lacks the heat, the vapor, of classic Black gay house music. It's cooler, like it's observing from the edges. Maybe that suits me. I'm not Black. I'm not a gay man – although I tried to be several times.

The good life to which 'Good Life' entices is still sexual, corporeal. And as is so often the case, it's a Black woman's voice that has to stand in for the ecstasy of the flesh. Often the Black woman's voice is required to perform itself to excess, to use gospel-trained pyrotechnics to worship flesh rather than spirit, like Loleatta Holloway on 'Love Sensation'. Or, in a different bag, Donna Summer's eight-minute orgasm on 'Love to Love You Baby'. Paris Grey does something else, something that is at once a seduction and a command. A power-bottom move.

∗

The space and time that good dance music creates can vaporise sexualities and genders. Whether you are gay or straight or none-of-the-above, when it comes to sex, your sexuality on the dance floor is something else. Everyone who lets the music in – lets the music move them, pass through them, fuck them – is queer for the dance. I was always queer for the dance, even if it took me a long time to figure out what this body was the rest of the time.

It was on the dance floor that I found, not so much a sexuality as a gender. I always loved to give myself over. I always wanted the rhythm to have its way with me. If there's dance music playing, I'm its bitch. For the longest time this body only felt like it could become itself while dancing. (Well, also while fucking, but that's another story.) For the longest time I felt the dance take me by the hand. It knew where it wanted to take me. I pulled away.

Twice, I made my life over. The first time was by emigration. I became a New Yorker. The second was by transition. I became a transsexual woman. I was looking for the good life. When I emigrated, it was for love of another. When I transitioned, it was for love of this body. The good life, I found, is just being where and what enables one to find some small possibility of ongoingness.

I'm playing remixes of 'Good Life' while I clean the kitchen. So much has changed since I first heard this song. I left Sydney for New York, for love. Twenty years later I came out, got separated, remade my version of the good life. Met someone else. Fell in love again. She's at work right now, while I Swiffer the floors.

So much has changed since I first heard this song. Including the song. The original still sounds like now to me, but now it's also part of other nows. Tastes change. Producers pull it apart and put it together again. The sub-bass registers of dance music expanded over the thirty-odd years since its first existence. Something like its signature is still there, in the remixes. The good ones, at least.

Maybe a remixed techno track appeals to me as it's how I feel about my own body. I took the technics that were available to me and used them for purposes for which they were not really designed. I hacked this body with hormones meant for other things to change its sex. And it worked, like a good techno track works. Make the empire's machines make a little of what we want for our needs and pleasures.

When a piece of pop music is interesting, maybe there are two things going on at once. Part of it is the way it provides a personal soundtrack to particular experiences. 'Good Life' condenses for me the lessons of the dance floor, which was once the only place I could go to get free. From there, eventually, the dance floor took me to the place I wanted to go – to my own good life. Hardly perfect – this Brooklyn rent doesn't pay itself. A life, all the same, which feels like it can be ongoing.

I honour this side of 'Good Life' by *not* listening to it. I'm listening instead to new sounds of now. Particularly on the dance floor. I want to dance to DJs

with a strong sense of now. They may weave some past into this present. After some track that showed up on Bandcamp yesterday, a snatch of classic Model 500, maybe. Or even 'Good Life.' I see so many of my generation caught in musical nostalgia doom-loops. Showing for reunion tours. I don't want my own past sold back to me as a boxed set.

The other side of songs that sticks with us is not so much our situation as their creators' situation. Pop music from the past is like a fossil from the bottom of the sea. It preserves the way the organism of music lived and loved and bred and fed in its time. 'Good Life' was a minor hit. There's a music video of Saunderson and Grey swanning around London. It was a bit of a path not taken by techno, much of which stayed in the small-business lane. Releases you had to know about to know about.

Techno is a music America never learned to love. It's Black music that was appropriated less by white Americans than by white Europeans. It got big in Berlin, in Northern England, in places where the Cold War industrial edifice collapsed into the era of 'neoliberal' liquidity. Techno was and remains the soundtrack for feeling one's way through the remaking by the digital not just of one's body, but of history. Techno is the sound of history uploading.

'Disco is audibly where the twenty-first century begins,' Kodwo Eshun wrote in *More Brilliant than the Sun*. I think of 'Do You Wanna Funk?' sung by Sylvester over a track by Patrick Cowley. It's Black, it's trans, it's (white) gay, and it's machine music. It's still the sound of now. Or almost. 'Good Life' is where the twenty-first century audibly begins for me. Meaning for me personally, for my own situation. But I'd venture it's as good a track as any to designate the beginning of a more pervasive sonic situation.

That its makers weren't gay maybe opened up a space for it to become sonically queer. Some backstory: At the end of the seventies, the disco boom was crushed by yet another wave of fetishising music made by straight white men with guitars. Disco went back underground and spawned house music – the sound of the Black gay body getting free – which in turn was appropriated back into straight white pop when everyone got bored with the pretensions of white boy guitar music. Meanwhile, pushing at the fringes of gay dance floors was the prospect of the *queer* dance floor. Something that might call for a different arrangement, both sonic and social, of nightlife.

My first attempt to be a gay man took place in Sydney in the early eighties. It wasn't a good time to be gay man who was femme. I was refused entry to the main gay clubs in Sydney on more than one occasion. The gay 'look' was the clone look. It was all about celebrating and performing gay masculinity. There wasn't much space on that dance floor for someone who felt more like a girl. The rise of a public and proud gay culture centred both whiteness and masculinity. So while I could be included under one heading (white), I wasn't under the other (too femme). I went back to doing straight(ish) boy drag in straight(er) clubs.

By the nineties things had improved somewhat in Sydney with the formation of Club Kooky and other parties, often run with the active participation of dykes and trans people. On my exploratory visits to New York in those years I found a similar spirit at Jackie 60, which was at Mother on Tuesday nights, or at The Pyramid, practically any time. A queer dance floor was coming into existence.

The late José Esteban Muñoz wrote a loving tribute to drag icon Kevin Aviance in *Cruising Utopia*. It's in an essay in which Muñoz also picks at his own relation as a gay man to enforced masculinity. I'd be a little less charitable about the role of drag in gay nightlife. I love drag, good drag at least, but there's a way that the drag queen performs femininity for a gay male dance floor so that the rest of the dance floor can disavow it. Masculinity makes no sense without something other to it. Drag produces the sign of the other so that gay masculinity can go back to its own pleasures.

I love all that, it just doesn't leave a lot of space for me, or for others whose gender and sexualities form themselves along different lines. And so: queer dance floors. Which include gay men, but don't centre gay masculinity and its performative structures. But what can a queer, as distinct from a gay, dance floor sound like? In Brooklyn, in the 2020s, it sounds more like techno than house music. By diverting the current of sonic culture away from house towards techno, a different kind of embodiment, a different kind of play, comes to the fore.

For me, personally, 'Good Life' is where the queer twenty-first century audibly begins. At least as a possibility. A queer life that includes trans bodies too. When I heard a sampled remix of 'Good Life' at the rave, and felt the crowd go off in knowing appreciation, I felt like this personal association of queerness with this track wasn't too much of a stretch. It took me thirty years to respond to that track's invitation, to find the good life. I did, eventually.

Nostalgia, Ultra: Ennui and Excess in Late Nineties Suburbia

Tabitha Lasley

For most of 2018, I worked in a takeaway. The work was hard, dirty, humbling. The staff lacked even basic employment rights. In lieu of these protections, we enjoyed certain privileges. Drug use was tolerated in the kitchen. We were allowed to play our own music. Each of us got an hour on the speaker. There were no restrictions; no standards enforced by head office. There was no head office. And if our customers disliked the shop's soundtrack – a hum of ambient, generalised profanity, augmented by intermittent cursing from the chefs – they never said.

There were no rules about repetition, either. If you wanted to spend your allocated hour playing the same song over and over again, until the words lost all meaning, you could. One of our chefs, a boy barely out of his teens, used to play *1999* by Charli XCX on repeat. The artwork shows her dressed up as Trinity from *The Matrix*, in black leather and rimless shades. The song is a list of Y2K ephemera – Nike Airs, MTV, Eminem, Britney Spears – set to rinky-dink pianos. It's nothing special. It sounds like a lot of songs that came out around that time.

Our chef played it so often, the lyrics are still emblazoned on my brain. On my hands and knees, scraping impacted cheese off the floor, or elbow-deep in greasy dishwater, scrubbing the blender's blades, I felt personally mocked by its refrain, the stated wish to go back to 1999. 'Hmm,' I'd think, as the chorus hit. 'You and me both, love.' Charli XCX would have been seven in 1999, making a lie of her line about driving around listening to Shady. But young people aren't immune to nostalgia. It's easier to romanticise a past you can barely recall.

Even those of us who can remember 1999 quite well have trouble accessing the details. It is easy to forget, now the news has come to resemble a rolling dystopian movie, that the late 1990s were a period of vague discontent. With hindsight, the closing years of the twentieth century look almost comically benign. The economy was in good shape, the political landscape stable. Studios were flush with cash, indie directors were given huge budgets to play with, musicians still made good money selling records. Artists should have been enthused about the future. Yet much of the cultural output creaked with unease, a subliminal desire to hit the brakes.

*

In 1998 Busta Rhymes released his masterpiece: *Extinction Level Event*. The album's cover is eerily prescient: it shows Manhattan engulfed in flames. Its most famous track, 'Gimme Some More', sounds like a transmission, beamed straight from the brain of Cassandra. On the surface, it's a breathless ode to excess, the lyrics a simple petition for more (more money, more things, more plaudits, more *life*), but the music undermines the message. Heard against the sample's skewed strings, an interpolation of the theme from *Psycho*, the words turn ominous, an end-times caution against needless accrual.

'Gimme Some More' shows the work of not one but two auteurs at the very top of their game. The video was shot by Hype Williams, then the go-to director for labels with money to burn. Williams's videos did not inform the nineties rap aesthetic, so much as invent it. His primary-coloured palette and low-slung shots still serve as a shorthand for the genre's salad days. Williams started out making ordinary videos for conventional musicians. His vision – warped both figuratively and literally by his trademark fish-eye lens – only reached its full potential when deployed by rappers prepared to get weird. Missy Elliot's early videos are a case in point. A lesser director might have tried to disguise her size, but Williams accentuated it, shooting her from below in unflattering clothes. In 'The Rain (Supa Dupa Fly)', she dons an inflatable bin bag and bike helmet, wet-look orange overalls, and the kind of long yellow shorts a boy explorer might wear. Her dancers jerk about; marionettes brought to life by malign powers. Other rappers and singers pop up for no reason, their appearances as irrelevant and unexplained as the cameos of old schoolfriends in a dream. At one point, Keisha from Total flashes a long, reptilian tongue at the camera. But it is a more prosaic scene that feels most unsettling. Missy sits atop a bright green hill, in a bright green jacket, legs splayed out. She plays with her hair and counts on her fingers; a grotesquely grown-up little girl.

Was Hype Williams frightened of children? It's a nice question. He certainly seemed to find something ghoulish about them, falling back on the creepy-kid trope more than once. 'Gimme Some More' opens with a small child, apparently knocked out under a tree. He lies on a luridly green lawn, tucked behind a white picket fence. A 1950s housewife, dressed in full Betty Draper regalia, picks her way towards him. Her approach is narrated by an adult Busta. In these lines, he relays advice given to him as a youth: if he can't be on the winning team, he must be the best himself. The woman draws near, and the child suddenly turns into a little blue monster with sharp yellow teeth. He chases her through her cartoon house, its walls curving and bending around her like the corridors of a funhouse. These sequences are interspersed with scenes of Busta in costume: as a record executive, a boxer, an old-school rapper in a sequinned tracksuit. At the turn of the century, music and athletics were still the most efficient avenues for a working-class Black man trying to access the American dream.

MTV played this video on heavy rotation all year. At the time, it struck me as a parable about ambition, the transformative effect of elbowing everyone out of the way in pursuit of your dreams. Once you know his band's back story, these lines read more like mitigation than manifesto. Busta Rhymes didn't want to be a solo artist; stardom was more or less thrust upon him. He started his career as part of the group Leaders of the New School. Protégés of Public Enemy, they enjoyed modest success. They disbanded because founding member Charlie Brown grew tired of Busta getting all the attention. Like a male Beyoncé, Busta's charisma and physical presence made his bandmates look like props. Unlike Beyoncé, he was distraught over the break-up. He begged Brown to reconsider. Brown refused to discuss it.

As for the *Leave It to Beaver* backdrop, that was just the spirt of the era. Concepts like 'affluenza' – a spiritual malaise borne of having too much stuff – were starting to gain purchase. In January 1999, HBO aired a new series: *The Sopranos*. It opened with Tony Soprano, a rich mobster living in an affluent

New Jersey suburb, complaining to his psychiatrist about the false promise of the American Project: 'The morning of the day I got sick I'd been thinking, it's good to be in something from the ground floor. I came too late for that. I know. But lately, I'm getting the feeling that I came in at the end. The best is over.'

Films had taken on a similarly gloomy tenor. Screenwriters were pitching suburbia as an existential hellscape; a hall-of-mirrors inversion of the small-town idyll. The true horror, they suggested, was an ordinary life. The year's most lauded films were nihilistic satires. One featured a man so fed up of his big house and boring wife, he resigns from his job and tries to seduce his teenage daughter's friend (*American Beauty*); the other a man so sick of his IKEA furniture, he blows his apartment up and starts fighting strange men in car parks (*Fight Club*). In one scene, he hectors his acolytes about their thwarted dreams, telling them: 'Advertising has us chasing cars and clothes, working jobs we hate so we can buy shit we don't need.'

Back then, the decline of the American Empire felt theoretical; the idea of its fall mildly thrilling. Two decades on, many pre-millennial predictions have come to pass, and though some of these films have aged remarkably well, they're no longer much fun to watch. By 2018, there was a sense we were witnessing the collapse of something; that the wheels were about to come off. My own life had slipped out from under my control, in tandem with this general downward slide. After a series of personal calamities, I'd moved back in with my mother. Having walked out on my career, I took a job at the takeaway, a service role that made no use of my talents, and *did* require skills I didn't have. I was supposed to be in a relationship with the proprietor, but I knew he didn't love me, not really. Like many ex-journalists, I had a manuscript languishing on my laptop. I didn't believe anyone would buy it.

Having grown up in the suburbs, I'd never found them sinister. They were a place of comfort for me, as the trees are for the birds. That winter, driving down endless, identical roads, delivering food to newbuilds so flimsy they looked more like stage sets than real houses, I decided David Lynch had a point. There was something spooky about these estates: the blankness of the buildings, the way they sprang up overnight, as if they'd somehow self-assembled. These streets looked so similar, I'd often get lost. Their extreme newness confounded my phone's GPS. The lack of any landmarks made navigation hard.

When I was a child, I used to devour those Choose Your Own Adventure books. They've since been supplanted by computer games; I'm not sure they publish them anymore. At the time, they were compulsive. You'd roll the dice and choose a path, guided by pure instinct. Sometimes, you'd make the right call and then you'd reach the end. Sometimes, you miscalculated, and then it was game over. The year I spent at the takeaway was like being trapped in one of my green-spined adventure books. I knew I'd made a mistake, taken a fateful wrong turn. I wanted to retrace my steps, go back to the beginning, start all over again.

With the depressive's tunnel vision, I obsessed over every poor choice and stupid decision. In retrospect, I can see certain things were beyond my control. The world has changed irrevocably since 1999. Younger millennials know this; they are well schooled in the facts of their frustrated progress: the 2008 crash, a contracting economy, spiralling property prices, standing student debt, an aging population, a demographic crunch. Older millennials tend to blame themselves. We were Thatcher's children, after all. We have retained enough of her mitochondrial DNA that we secretly believe everything wrong with our lives is our fault.

As I mopped the floor and stacked dishes to the strains of Charli XCX, I felt a split in my perception open up. I had lived through 1999. I knew it wasn't a prelapsarian age, before we learned to want. Already, we were yearning for the recent past, convinced our best days were behind us. We went to 'old-school' nights, where they played hardcore songs released a few years earlier. We moaned that drugs weren't as good as they used to be; music wasn't as good as it used to be; the scene wasn't as good as it used to be. These last two charges were subjective; the first just wasn't true. Mitsubishis, the most ubiquitous pills of the era, were stronger than anything available in 1988. Even so: it would be hard to argue that things have improved. Broadly speaking, life *was* better twenty years ago. Citizens slept easy in their beds. Young people weren't as sick; they didn't hate themselves as thoroughly. Art was bolder because artists were given the funds to experiment, and the latitude to mess up.

Bravery is a boom-time luxury. Faced with an uncertain future, the temptation is to cling to what you know, to what has worked for you in the past. I felt some sympathy: for our chef and his repetitious choices; for modern musicians and their endless riffs on the same formula. There is safety in ceaseless repetition, in each day being exactly like the next. Anyway, I wasn't in a position to judge. I was hiding behind my dead-end job, my relationship with a man who didn't like me very much. I might have stayed there forever, making minute adjustments to my manuscript, getting lost on featureless estates. Except occasionally, life forces your hand.

One day, I walked out of the shop to find my boyfriend-slash-boss sitting in his car, texting another woman. He hurled his phone into the footwell. His eyes seethed with panic. I knew then that I had reached a juncture. I could pretend I hadn't seen, turn around, and walk back into the shop. Or I could act like a grown-up for once. So I gathered up the last vestiges of my self-respect, grabbed my bag from the counter, and took my cab fare from the till.

'I'm going home,' I told him. 'You can close up without me tonight.'

In fact, he couldn't, because I'd walked off with the keys. That's a metaphor. Or something. As it turned out, he couldn't keep the shop open without me either. Not long after I left, the business shut down. So often, men discard the women they depend on. They only realise what they've done when the superstructure of their lives comes crashing down. It's like knocking the supporting walls of a house through. You can't start crying when the ceiling caves in. For a while, my ex would send miserable texts, always late at night. And though I felt a pang of survivor's guilt every time, this was one impulse to go back I managed to resist.

I never saw him again. I never saw the shop again, either. Sometimes, I catch a glimpse of the street where it stood, as I speed past the town, on my way to the outlet village, located at the next junction. I am still enough of a sucker that advertising has me buying shit I do not need. All I can say in my defence is that I no longer work a job I hate to afford it.

I still listen to old rap in the car: Q Tip; Mos Def; Busta Rhymes. *Extinction Level Event* sounds even better, now that we're doomed to live in interesting times. 'Gimme Some More' feels loaded with portent; the auditory equivalent of those wild-eyed men who stride up and down the high street in sandwich boards, warning heedless shoppers about the end of days. When you've never had it so good, the lyrics seem to say, where is there to go but down? Of course, at the turn of the century, we couldn't have known for sure. But we were about to find out.

Hot Legs

Wendy Erskine

The summer of 1983, I went to stay with my French pen pal for a month. I had a Lady Di haircut, I didn't know much French, and I was fourteen. Tracie Young, who had sung backing vocals on the Jam's 'Beat Surrender' the previous year before going on to have her own hits, was my favourite pop star. The article in *No.1* magazine, where she met her idol, Paul Young, and told him how she checked his horoscope every day, was to my mind a work of great literature. I forgot to bring anything to read on the trip, so I made do with the two English-language books I found on the shelf in my Paris bedroom: *Fat Is a Feminist Issue* by Susie Orbach and *The Prophecies of Nostradamus*. When I wasn't being introduced to a psychoanalytic dissection of the ideologies of eating, I was pondering how the young lion would overcome the older one on the field of battle and pierce his eyes through a golden cage so he died a cruel death.

I've never really gone in at all for the idea about French people being stylish. That said, it dawned on me quickly that my French pen pal's family were pretty cool customers. There were two older brothers: the one with very blue eyes was into '50s rock 'n' roll, and the other had a crew cut and liked King Sunny Adé. One July afternoon, I stood in a shop with my pen pal and her cousin, staring at a wall of singles. At number one was 'L'Italiano' by Toto Cutugno. My pen pal's cousin pointed at one of the 7-inches and asked if I liked it. It was Rod Stewart and the single was 'Baby Jane'. I hated 'Baby Jane'. So I instantly said, *non*. She lifted 'Baby Jane' from its plastic slot to examine the cover, its multiple versions of lovelorn Rod in black PVC. She said that I must in fact like him because he was English. Actually, *non*, I repeated.

I couldn't explain how he was someone to be laughed at, how in the *Kenny Everett Video Show* parody of him, his bum inflated over the course of the dopey song 'Da Ya Think I'm Sexy?' until he took off into the air. My French didn't extend to that. ('Da Ya Think I'm Sexy?' is, it has to be said, not really very sexy. It might seem all black satin sheets, Jackie Collins, and zipless fucks, but it's tentative and reasonably angst-ridden. She's alone, he's nervous. Her heart is pounding, his lips are dry. She points out that if they are going to pursue things, then she needs to borrow a dime so that she can phone her mother. He, unfortunately, doesn't have any coffee or milk.) Instead I feigned an interest in French singers and bands I'd never heard of, lifting records, pretending to read the notes. *Je n'aime pas Rod Stewart. Il est très awful.*

And then I remembered that I liked the video for 'Hot Legs'.

'Hot Legs' is what Rod Stewart called one of his 'shagging songs'. You know the sort: lines about being well-equipped, keeping pencils sharp, jet-black suspender belts, pussies being whipped and so on, and so on. It was the second single from 1977's *Foot Loose and Fancy Free*, one of a series of '70s albums including *Atlantic Crossing* and the platinum *A Night on the Town*. *Foot Loose* is a bit of a mix. There's a psychedelic Motown cover, big ballads with the element of existential questioning Rod often favours. 'I Was Only Joking' is rueful and thoughtful. It offers a meta-take, a singer alienated from a crowd that doesn't understand. And then there is 'Hot Legs' in which, at the endearingly specific time of a quarter to four, Rod is importuned by a woman.

That's a common motif in Rod-associated songs, from the Faces onwards. Hapless guys are waylaid from the righteous path by sirens. In 'Had Me a Real Good Time', someone is simply, innocently, cycling through his neighbourhood, minding his own business, when he is invited by a high-class girl to a party. In 'Maggie May', he would be back in school, of course, were it not for that older woman. 'Hot Legs' is similar, but this time she is young and possibly still in school. She may be alluring but, like Rita in 'Stay with Me', she will need to disappear when her company is no longer required. Get up! Get out!

*

By the time I was standing in the Parisian shop, looking at the French singles of 1983, I had seen, while walking to school, a woman trying to escape from a car. I had watched as a man dragged her back into it by her hair. I had read, along with everyone else, the proto-fan fiction a classmate had written based on *The Stud*. The handwriting might have been neat and loopy but the content was X-rated. I had had a Santa Claus in a shopping centre ask me when I sat on his knee if he could have a nice kiss. A proper kiss. I had danced around at a twelfth birthday party to a song that was on repeat, 'You've Gotta Be a Hustler if You Wanna Get On' by Sue Wilkinson, sung in a breathy Home Counties voice, stressing the imperative of using sex as a career-advancement strategy. The world didn't seem a terribly pristine place.

In some ways wasn't that just great? It was a thrill to read samizdat sleaze, sitting on the floor of a school cloakroom, surrounded by duffle coats. In other ways it was horrible. It was not pleasant to have some man's eyes slide over your legs and knee socks when you were on a bus. In some ways it was confusing: the joy and delight in songs whose sentiments in the real world would be reprehensible. Rock 'n' roll, the irresponsible genre. Perhaps too irresponsible: nowadays Rod has apparently dropped 'Tonight's the Night', 'Da Ya Think I'm Sexy?', and 'Hot Legs' from his sets.

And yet and yet and yet. It remains a video I love. It never fails to put me in a better mood. Director Bruce Gowers, responsible for many other videos including 'Bohemian Rhapsody', 'Stayin' Alive', and Prince's '1999', might have intended something cheeky, cheery, and sexy, which spoke to an ordinary guy Everyman. The band are in blue-collar luxe workwear and jumpsuits. There are garages, barns, yards: quotidian spots. There is a 'hot bird'. But more than that, it would seem, is going on.

It opens with a kick, *in medias res*. It's an overcast day but Rod and the boys are full of exuberance as they ride into town on the roof of the car. And that town is Piru, in Ventura County, California. It's been used as a film location on many occasions, from the 1954 version of *A Star Is Born* to the more recent *Lucky*, starring Harry Dean Stanton. Rod's in dungarees but they have the addition of a little belt with a kind of Gucci snaffle bit. The ebullient mood is tempered somewhat by a slab of dull-looking mountain behind them and the overcast weather.

Then comes a very striking shot. The band are walking in a line, spaghetti western fashion, the scrubland and crags behind them. They proceed along railway tracks but in the foreground is something, immobile, lying across the metal. It's the legs of a woman and she is wearing high heels. The rest of her is out of shot. It looks like the body of someone who has been murdered or the legs of a shop mannequin, abandoned in this bleak spot. Certainly, the men aren't too interested or disturbed. They simply walk on by, apart from the one guy who has to step over the legs to continue on his way. The song might be cheerily horny, but on this railway line in Piru things are decidedly not.

It's rumoured that the legs (and on a couple of occasions, an upper body) which appear at various times in this video belong to Jenilee Harrison, who went on to play the character of Jamie Ewing Barnes in Dallas from 1984 to 1986. I can't confirm this, but having looked at pictures of her legs in various photographs and movie stills, they strike me as pretty similar. I always notice people's legs. In my own writing – short stories – I am probably more likely to describe someone's legs than their face: whether they are, you know, palely muscled, or twitching, or veined. I notice when women have Paula Rego–style legs: strong, thick, powerful. Sometimes when I look at my own legs and the shape of them in heels and tight trousers, I am reminded of that precise moment in *Animal Farm* when the pigs begin to walk on their hind legs. That's why I don't often wear heels and tight trousers. I marvel at the woman's legs in the sculpture by F. E. Williams, *Woman in a Bomb Blast*. Propelled backwards by the blast, her legs are as elegant and slender as those of a model on a packet of tights. That's what comes to mind first, for me, rather than any commentary on Northern Ireland. Not long ago, I saw Maarten van Heemskerck's *Ecce Homo Triptych*. Jesus is placed beside Pilate, governor of Judaea. What struck me most of all was the way Pilate and Jesus had exactly the same legs, although Pilate was wearing red tights. There was an identical degree of curve from the knee, the same prominent shin bones.

In the next scene of 'Hot Legs', the legs are no longer on the railway tracks. One lies flat on the ground, while the other is bent. Rod is filmed through the triangle this makes. He smirks, closes his eyes in bliss. This particular frame-within-a-frame has some pedigree. In *The Graduate*, Benjamin Braddock, dressed in suit and tie, is framed by Mrs Robinson's bare leg. In the movie poster for *For Your Eyes Only*, 007 is there under tanned legs in high heels and skimpy pants. Yesterday I saw on a T-shirt the Grim Reaper framed by the legs of a sexy skeleton in go-go boots.

But then, disembodied women's legs aren't anything particularly new in art either, are they? There are the two pairs of legs, conjoined beneath the moon, in Max Ernst's *Men Shall Know Nothing of This*; and Jim Dine's *Walking Dream with Four Foot Clamp*, which shows nineteen legs. Also appearing in the painting are tools like a spanner. In some ways, it has the same 'legs-plus-work' aesthetic as Rod's video. And what about Allen Jones with his disembodied legs in high heels, and Laurie Simmons with her cameras and houses on top of a pair of women's legs?

But what this video – with its erotic and unerotic elements – most reminds me of is *Pauline Bunny*, Sarah Lucas's assemblage of tights stuffed with kapok, a mid-century wooden chair, and some clamps. As in the Max Ernst painting, there are two sets of legs, but in *Pauline Bunny*, one pair wears stockings. The tights are stretched over the chair, integrating functionality. And there's no head, just another set of legs, secured with clamps. (I made something a little similar myself as a kid, out of stuffed tights, except my creation was dressed in a track suit and had a smiley face. It sat in my room for months. I called it *Big Bertha*.)

The legs in the video are again used to frame Rod, but they are positioned in a reverse composition. They remain immobile, still as a mannequin, still as death. It will come as little surprise that all along, the legs have been wearing fishnet tights. First popular with showgirls and flappers in the 1920s, fishnets have been a hit with all kinds of people ever since: punks, goths, skin girls, dancers, acrobats – anyone really, who wants to liven up a dowdy outfit with a little frisson. Fishnet tights invariably appear in the stock photos used to accompany news stories about kerb-crawling, the kind of images that purport to be illustrative but are in fact there for titillation. The images are never of the punters, looking in their rear-view windows, pulling on the handbrake, pressing down the window. No, they are of shapely women in bomber jackets, high heels, and fishnets, leaning into the car, negotiating terms.

What fishnets do is make legs look good. They give a black line that offers definition, but then the squares distort around any curves of knee or calve, accentuating the shape. So yes, of course, for so many reasons the legs here in the video are going to be wearing fishnets.

Other aspects of the video destabilise the hotness. One is the number of dogs that appear: dusty, good-natured dogs sniffing around. At one point, Rod half-addresses a lascivious line about a jet-black suspender belt to an unperturbed old mutt. During the middle eight, the guitarist proceeds down the railway track, laughing, doing a Chuck Berry duckwalk. The legs are nowhere to be seen, but he is followed by a crowd of children, a few awkward, but most smiling. One wears a T-shirt saying Piru.

But let me tell you about my favourite person in the whole video. I'm suspicious of first-person narratives. They're always unreliable. Just like lyric poems – unreliable too. No matter how circumspect and supposedly frank and transparent the story is supposed to be, it's always compromised. I like any writer who acknowledges that, particularly one who builds into a first-person narrative an alternative perspective on the central consciousness and its worldview. In Megan Nolan's *Acts of Desperation*, the narrator tells a story of female desire and power and love and mistreatment. I loved it. At one point, in comes an ex-boyfriend Reuben to say, 'You always think your pain is the most painful. You always think it's uniquely awful.' Such alternative perspectives puncture the hermetic dimension of the narrative. There is a character not unlike this in the Rod Stewart video. He is there from the beginning and cut to repeatedly. He's a fairly old man, self-possessed, at ease, wearing a grey sweatshirt and soft hat, his legs crossed composedly. He looks bored, and he turns his head away from Rod's antics – as if to say, *I can't be bothered with all this nonsense.*

At a certain point in the video, the camera pulls back and for the first time we see a body attached to the legs. There is still no face – we see the woman from the back – but she has long brown, highlighted hair, a white top, and blue shorts. Again her legs are used to frame Rod. But then we cut to another shot, and now the legs are framing someone else: the old man. He turns his head away in ennui and maybe disdain.

The legs again are immobile by the end of the video. Rod actually touches one of them, in the way one might a piece of guttering. *I love you honey*, he says, and looks upwards into the dark crotch of fishnet. At this moment, there's something I imagine. And it's the face of the old man, its look of slight contempt. Then there's a montage of various leg shots before the guys drive back out of Piru, still on the roof of the car, passing a haulage depot on the way.

In my suitcase, when I went to stay with my pen pal, was a bottle of the legendary '80s potion, Sun In. It promised Californian beachy blonde through spray-on hydrogen peroxide action. But it reliably turned everyone's hair – including mine – a shade of brassy yellow. My Lady Di haircut grew out. And so, whether I liked Rod Stewart or not, by the end of the trip I looked like him.

NOTES ON CONTRIBUTORS

CIARAN CARSON (1948–2019) was a poet and writer of fiction and non-fiction who was born in Belfast. He was the founder of the Seamus Heaney Centre, Queen's University Belfast, author of nine books of poetry and four prose works, and the winner of several awards including the Irish Times Irish Literature Prize, the T. S. Eliot Prize, and the Forward Prize for Best Poetry Collection for Breaking News in 2003.

BRIAN DILLON is an Irish writer based in London. His books include *Affinities* (2023), *Suppose a Sentence* (2020), *Essayism* (2017), and *In the Dark Room* (2005). His writing has appeared in the *New Yorker*, *New York Review of Books*, *London Review of Books*, the *Guardian*, and *Granta*.

WENDY ERSKINE has written two short-story collections, *Sweet Home* and *Dance Move* (The Stinging Fly Press). For PVA Books, she edited *well I just kind of like it*, an anthology about art and the home.

AINGEALA FLANNERY is a novelist and short-story writer. Her fiction debut, *The Amusements*, was published by Penguin Sandycove in 2022 and won the Kerry Group Novel of the Year 2023 and the John McGahern Prize. She lives in Dublin.

PETER GEOGHEGAN is an Irish writer and journalist based in London. His most recent book, *Democracy for Sale: Dark Money and Dirty Politics*, was a *Sunday Times* bestseller.

NOTES ON CONTRIBUTORS

COLIN GRAHAM is Professor of English at Maynooth University.

M. JOHN HARRISON's first book, *The Committed Men*, was published in 1971 and his most recent, the memoir *Wish I Was Here*, in 2023. He lives in Shropshire.

TABITHA LASLEY was a journalist for ten years. Her memoir, *Sea State*, was shortlisted for the Gordon Burn Prize and the Portico Prize and longlisted for the Rathbones Folio Prize. It was a *Guardian* and *Times* Book of the Year (2021). Her work has appeared in *Granta*, *Esquire*, the LRB, and *The Paris Review*.

DECLAN LONG is an art critic and lecturer, based in Dublin. He is the author of *Ghost-Haunted Land: Contemporary Art and Post-Troubles Northern Ireland* (2017).

JAYNE A. QUAN is the author of *All This Happened, More or Less*. They are currently based in Los Angeles with their wife and two cats.

McKENZIE WARK is the author, among other things, of *Reverse Cowgirl* (Semiotexte), *Raving* (Duke University Press), and *Love and Money, Sex and Death* (Verso). She lives in Brooklyn and teaches at the New School.

SYDNEY WEINBERG's writing has appeared in *The Dublin Review*, *Tolka*, *The Stinging Fly*, *The Tangerine*, *Banshee*, *gorse*, and others. She was longlisted for the Deborah Rogers Foundation Award in 2020.

IMAGE LIST

p. 15   Concert ticket stub for Echo and the Bunnymen. Courtesy of the author.

pp. 58–59   Iggy Pop of the Stooges during a performance at the Cincinnati Pop Festival at Crosley Field, Cincinnati, Ohio, 13 June 1970. Photo: Tom Copi/Michael Ochs Archive/Getty Images.

pp. 74–75   Photos by Luke McManus taken at The Night Before Larry Got Stretched, The Cobblestone, Smithfield, Dublin, October 2021.

p. 79   Flyer for *Oral Blessings*. Courtesy of the author.

p. 113   Courtesy of the author.

p. 144   Photo of column covered in layers of posters advertising concerts, Kastanienallee, Berlin. Photo: PVA Books.